Volunteer:

WITH THE POOR IN PERU

by
Jeff Thielman
and
Raymond A. Schroth, S.J.

PAULIST PRESS
New York ■ Mahwah, N.J.

Library of Congress Cataloging-in-Publication Data

Thielman, Jeff, 1963–
    Volunteer: with the poor in Peru/by Jeff Thielman and Raymond A. Schroth.
      p. cm.
    ISBN 0–8091–3243–5 (pbk.)
    1. Social work with children—Peru—Tacna. 2. Socially handicapped children—Peru—Tacna. 3. Thielman, Jeff, 1963–
4. Youth volunteers in social service—Peru—Tacna—Biography. 5. Cristo Rey Center for the Working Child (Tacna, Peru)
6. Boston College. International Volunteer Program. I. Schroth, Raymond A. II. Title.
HV887.P42T338 1991
361.7'092—dc20
[B]   91–9652
                                            CIP

Published by Paulist Press
997 Macarthur Boulevard
Mahwah, New Jersey 07430

Printed and bound in the
United States of America

Contents

(Photo by Marianne Persianoff)

Introduction

When my generation graduated from college in the 1950s, our idea of going into a way of life where we could serve other people was to become a social worker or a teacher, or join the F.B.I. or the C.I.A. Yes, we could become a priest or a nun; but, at that time, most of us who were going to do that had made the decision right after high school and were already well along toward ordination or final vows, and those of us who either had decided against the religious life or were waiting for a clearer sign often turned toward government vocations as a way of expending our energies on behalf of the common good. Somehow we shared an understanding of government as the protector of the people, an understanding strengthened—some would say distorted—by the cold war, which divided the world into two opposing camps and thus gave a noble, dramatic, and realistic purpose to those like myself who were assigned to artillery units in Germany and those who, to put it bluntly, became cops and spies.

After my military service, I went on to two of the other "service" professions—teaching and the priesthood. There were forty-four novices in my class when I entered in 1957 (fifteen of whom are still in), and I am sure that when asked why we had come in, all would give some version of the same answer Jeff Thielman would give when asked why he went to Peru: "To help people." It was the best use of the talents God had given us, a way of achieving

1

"his will" on earth by doing "his" work. And, if we stuck with it and things worked out, there would be that "hundredfold" reward which Jesus promises his disciples in the gospel, the smiles on the faces of the children, the students, the families, the poor, sick and dying for whom we had become channels of grace.

Within a few years, we witnessed a radical change in the way American Christians viewed the world and in how they would insert themselves into that world in the process of both achieving God's will and accomplishing their own salvation.

On the political level, the Vietnam War and the moral questions it raised about our national character, plus the influence of the emerging counter-culture of the 1960s, severely undermined the confidence the young once had not just in the government but in all institutions.

But another reason for the change was the gradual breaking down, in theological understanding, of the distinction between the so-called sacred and secular realms. In our new view of the secular world, it was seen not as opposed to the religious sphere, waiting to be "baptized," but rather as good in itself, as already "graced." To reinforce this, the documents of Vatican II, specifically the 1965 Pastoral Constitution on the Church in the Modern World, proclaimed that "The joys and the hopes, the griefs and anxieties of the men of this age, especially those who are poor or in any way afflicted, these too are the joys and hopes, the griefs and anxieties of the follower of Christ."

Meanwhile, President John F. Kennedy, the "Catholic candidate" with a thoroughly secular education and intellectual framework, had anticipated this theme in the last line of his 1960 inaugural address: ". . . here on earth God's work must truly be our own." In other words, secular work, rebuilding human society, is the same thing as "God's work."

The embodiment of this spirit was the Peace Corps,

which immediately tapped the idealism of thousands of young men and women who, only a few years before, might have gone into teaching or the religious life.

In a very short thirty years, the relationship between higher education and public service has changed so profoundly that by the time he or she graduates, nearly every student will have had at least some opportunity—whether one accepts it or not—to spend some time "helping people": as a weekly volunteer in some soup kitchen, AIDS hospice or community action program, building homes or schools during the summer or Christmas break in Appalachia or Latin America, or committing oneself to a year or two in the Peace Corps, the Jesuit Volunteer Corps, or one of the many international volunteer programs sponsored by various religious orders.

For example, Boston College, where our story begins, in 1989 sent sixty-three graduates into the Jesuit Volunteer Corps, which involves living in a small community and taking on social projects in the inner city, on Indian reservations and in Alaska. And twenty-eight students entered its International Volunteer Program. Most of these young people had already worked in B.C. volunteer programs and taken courses taught by Father Julio Giulietti, S.J. as part of the Faith, Peace and Justice academic minor established in 1983. Father Julio writes on the board the first day of class, "Information without knowledge— knowledge without understanding—understanding without commitment—is useless."

I first met Jeff in November 1989. That summer I had gone to Peru to study the political situation and had published a report in *Commonweal*. Jeff, meanwhile, had returned from three years in Peru with a very long manuscript, based on his diaries, about his experience. At the invitation of Paulist Press, we worked together to bring forth *Volunteer*.

Obviously, for the project to succeed, we had to both like and trust one another, and we have shared the conviction from the start that in fairness to the readers, especially the readers who may become volunteers, we would report the failures, the despair, as well as the "hundredfold," and that we would not paper-over the faults of our volunteer. So we have left in Jeff's occasional obtuseness, his adolescent behavior, his drinking and swearing. I know from interviewing people who worked with Jeff that not everyone loved him all the time. They have described him as "driven," a "charmer," a "bulldozer." But, as one said, "It was hard to stay mad at him"; he had never known a young person to overcome so many obstacles, to accomplish so much in so short a time.

Raymond A. Schroth, S.J.
July 10, 1990

We are grateful to several friends who helped us by reading this manuscript and offering criticisms: Kate Adams, Chris Doyle, Paul Brant, S.J., Bob McCarty, S.J., Ben Birnbaum, Jim Mroz, and Tom Bruenn. We thank our families and friends, particularly Jeff's parents and Jill Alper, and the Jesuit and lay co-workers at Tacna, for their support and cooperation.

We dedicate this book to the poor of Peru, with the hope and prayer that someday, somehow, they may achieve a little more justice, a little more peace.

Prologue

It's mid-February 1989, in my grandparents' home in Barefoot Bay, Florida. The weather is warm but crisp and very comfortable—sort of like late spring in my native New England. Gram is cooking breakfast, Gramp is still asleep. I lie in my bed thinking, wondering, dreaming. It's hard to believe I'm in the U.S.A.

Spread out on the desk beside the word processor are my diaries from Peru. Some people always remember birthdays, or the dates of famous battles, or their wedding anniversary. I'll always remember October 19, 1985, the day I left for Peru, and February 4, 1989, the day I came home. Scattered on the bed next to me are snapshots of Ceferino, Andres, Jose Luis, Kickers, and other photos of the mothers. The pictures came back from Fotomat yesterday, but I couldn't look at them right away. I waited until Gram and Gramp went to bed. I wanted to look at shots of my last few days in Peru alone.

I jog in the morning and say hello to people, and all I can think about is Peru. Tacna, Peru! Who the hell ever heard of it? Who wants to hear about it? Who wants to know what it's like to be a volunteer in the third world and be with the poor?

It's too hard to explain to people. Everywhere I go my grandparents' friends are nice and polite. They congratulate me for helping the poor. In fact, everything here is nice, orderly. The water in the shower is hot. The water in the community pool is just the right temperature. My room in my grandparents' house is temperature-controlled. The TV has over forty stations. The golf course in front of the house is perfectly manicured. We drink spring water, sold in a supermarket. The refrigerator is always full. I enjoy chatting with my grandfather's friends at the coffee shop; they look forward to seeing me—a young face.

Don't get me wrong. It's good to be home. It's great to talk politics with my grandfather again. My father flies down from Connecticut to see me. My mother comes the following week. But I'm not ready to journey to Connecticut, to face everything from my past that awaits me there.

Before I am ready, I have to sort out what has happened to me over the last three years.

I

"Gringo Chancho"

"You miserable little shit!" I yelled in my angry, foul-mouthed English at Juan Carlos, the eleven year old Peruvian boy whom I had grabbed in a terrible moment of uncontrollable rage. "You ungrateful little rat. I built this place for rotten little scum like you—and look what you do to me!"

It was Saturday afternoon religion class—they were supposed to be making collages—at the Cristo Rey Center for the Working Child, a small, primitive, storefront building on Bolognesi Street in the town of Tacna (with a growing population of over 160,000) in southern Peru; and I had lost control.

Halfheartedly supervised by a group of middle-class students from the local Jesuit high school, where I had come to work as a Boston College International Volunteer, these twelve poor eight to twelve year old street kids—shoeshine boys, car washers, newsboys, and thieves—had been cutting out pictures from magazines and arranging them on three white boards in sections to represent good and evil.

My hope was that this artistic exercise would serve as a moral lesson, enable them to conceptualize more clearly the differences between right and wrong.

But six of their unruly friends, whom I had sent away earlier, had returned and were throwing rocks at the building. I went outside, yelled at them, and threatened to call

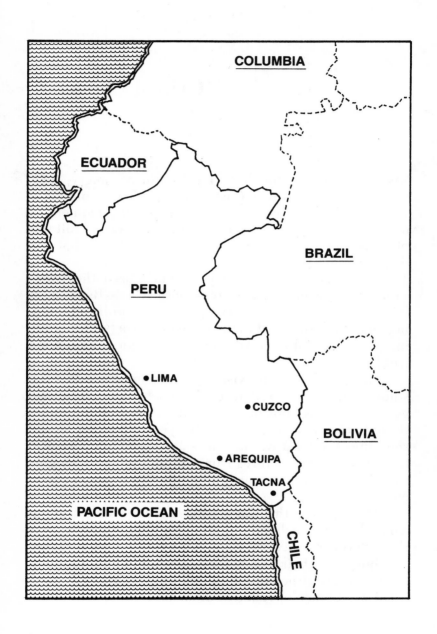

the police—like those pathetic, intimidated men and women in every American neighborhood who have lost control of their own turf and are reduced to hollow threats all children know they are impotent to carry out.

"Go ahead, gringo. Call the police. We're really scared." They mocked me. A car full of seniors whom I taught at the high school drove up, saw that I looked foolish, and joined in shouting and honking their horn.

Back inside the classroom, the kids had quit work and were throwing rocks at one another. I tried to silence them with a final class prayer—the last refuge of a teacher who has lost control of a class of supposedly "good" Catholic kids—and told them all to go home; but they flocked around me, groping in my pants for fruit and candy. Then I saw him.

Juan Carlos stood in the corner, urinating against the wall. The goddamned little punk—he was doing it to make me mad.

I seized him and lifted him off the ground shaking him angrily in the air—as his penis, protruding from his unzipped fly, wiggled in front of his giggling friends. I wanted to rub his nose in his urine, but I dragged him across the room toward the door, his pants and shirt ripped from some fight years ago, his fly still open and his defiant penis still exposed, and dumped him outside on the street.

I ordered everyone else, including the high school students, to go home. Then I got a damp rag and began to wipe Juan Carlos' urine off the wall.

Out in the street, the kids renewed their barrage of stones against the Center walls as they chanted, "Gringo Chancho! Gringo Chancho!" (Gringo Pig!)

For this I had postponed law school, left my family, my friends, and a girl I loved.

For this.

9

II

The Opening Days

When we first flew into Tacna on October 19, 1985, the Center for the Working Child was in no way part of my future.

After graduating from Boston College, where I had been president of the student government and, like the rest of my class, had passed four years having a great time, I spent a week sailing with my roommates in the Virgin Islands. Then I worked for the summer in the Massachusetts State House, and in the evenings I waited tables at Boston's historic Faneuil Hall Marketplace. To people who knew me simply as observers, who had perceived little of the internal and family struggle that had been going on over the past several months, I was one more "successful" B.C. grad headed for a good law school and maybe a political career.

With two other volunteers from B.C., Bonnie Sweeney and Leigh Shelton, I was to teach at Colegio Cristo Rey, the all-boys Jesuit school of six hundred and forty students (two hundred in high school) in Tacna, Peru's southernmost city, right above the Chilean border. My assignments: English, history and religion, plus coach basketball. Although I had done six weeks in Madrid in 1983, I still knew very little Spanish; and although I had grown up trying to play sports like any American boy, I'm afraid I knew nothing about basketball.

Tacna first struck me as isolated in the middle of the

world's longest, driest, desert valley, and it is known as one of the worst towns for robberies, but it has its charms.

The peaks of the Andes—Tutupaca and Yucamani to the north and the snow-capped Tacora to the east—loom on the horizon. In the center of town, the governor's office, city hall and the cathedral, designed by the firm of the French architect Eiffel, face each other across Plaza de Armas. Tall palm trees shade the city-long east-west main street, Avenida Bolognesi, with its wide center walkway, named for a hero in Peru's War of the Pacific against Chile (1879–1884). Indeed, much of the town's historical identity has its roots in that war: Tacna was captured by Chile in 1880 and remained part of Chile until it returned to Peru in a plebiscite in 1929.

Well dressed businessmen—criollos, light-skinned Peruvians with Spanish blood—mingle with the dark, squat Aymara Indians. Indian women in their several layers of brightly-colored dresses and round European hats hawk their fruits and vegetables, cigarettes and chewing gum on the street. And, I discovered, there were lots of Italians in town—Lombardis, Rossis and Gneccos.

Measured by familiar American standards, the town reaches about thirty blocks to the east and west and the north and south, with parks, plazas, schools and convents clustered around the cathedral. The sports stadium, which seats ten thousand, is about ten blocks north of the center, and the bleak, industrial zones reach out to the northeast. It has a clean but not necessarily modern hospital, a small university, and, probably as a legacy of the Chilean war, several military posts. These were expanded in a 1975 mobilization, at the threat of a Chilean invasion that didn't take place. Today military symbols are emblazoned on the surrounding hillsides as evidence of the military's clout.

Beyond the center of town, in the contraband markets, the entrepreneurs of Peru's dynamic "underground" economy turn a fast profit selling radios, televisions and cameras smuggled in untaxed from the town of Arica on

11

the other side of the Chilean border. To some economists, like Fernando DeSoto, author of *The Other Path*, this "underground" economy is the potential source of Peru's revitalization; to others, it is a symptom of its economic chaos.

Spread out on the perimeter of the city, especially on the sandy slopes of the hills to the northwest, sprawl the teeming, miserable barrios—which the Peruvian government, in an attempt to disguise a social problem by giving it an optimistic name, has designated "pueblos jovenes," or young towns. Since World War II, the Indians have fled the poverty, ignorance, and, recently, violence of the countryside; they have literally "invaded" abandoned land around the major cities in the middle of the night and set up straw huts which, over the years, they sometimes ingeniously develop into decent, suburban-style homes.

But even when a municipality eventually responds to their presence by stringing some lights or sending some social workers, these peasants must struggle daily to survive, as they carry water from a stream or buy it from a passing tank truck, beg or hustle coins in the city streets, eventually replace their thatch walls with cinderblocks, and escort their little children to makeshift schools.

The Jesuit school where we were assigned to work, however, was far from makeshift. Father Fred J. Green (sixty-three in 1985), a California Jesuit who had become a priest partly in reaction to the violence he both witnessed and wrought as a Marine bomber pilot in the Solomon Islands during World War II, founded the school in 1962, just three years after he and another American Jesuit arrived as parish priests in 1959.

In priest-poor Peru, the great majority of the clergy, particularly the more progressive priests, are from other countries. Some are diocesan priests from America, Canada, England and Ireland who come for a set number of years (for example, five years), sponsored by the Society

12

Top: A woman and her daughter beside their *choza* (thatched hut) outside Tacna. In the distant background are dwellings being built by Habitat for Humanity. Bottom: Children shining shoes and selling newspapers on the streets of Tacna. The boys worked an average of eight hours a day.

of Saint James in Boston, and then return to their home parishes reeducated by their taste of the third world. Others are members of religious orders, like the Jesuits, who both teach in the universities in Lima and have established a network of primary and secondary schools throughout the country.

From a one-room, flea-infested building, with help from United States and local businessmen, Father Fred developed Cristo Rey into a thriving, highly respected institution with a science laboratory, an audio-visual center, several concrete soccer and basketball courts, a perfectly manicured soccer field, and a complete farm with animals, fruit trees, and crops.

Every Monday morning at 8:20, the boys, dressed in gray and white uniforms, stand in formation and click their heels to attention as the band plays the Peruvian national anthem and the "United States Marine Hymn"—a rousing piece which every American boy of my father's generation had memorized during World War II. Father Fred of course had not made the youth of Tacna learn the "Marine Hymn," but their Peruvian music teacher had discovered this stirring march and taught it to them nonetheless. And it caught the spirit of the man who gave his spirit to the school.

We first arrived at Tacna at dusk, met by the volunteers we would be replacing, and by Father Fred, who struck me then merely as a slight, shy, balding man who gave no clue that he was beginning to tire of a task at which he had labored for so long. The semi-darkness clouded any sense of where we were; we saw only miles and miles of sand and, in the distance, what looked like rows and rows of bombed-out shacks.

After a hasty liturgy, of which, in spite of the six weeks I had once spent trying to learn Spanish in Spain, I understood not a word, they whisked us to a comfortable, middle-class home for a dinner geared to the tastes of newly-arrived gringos—pizza, bread, pie, wine and ice cream.

14

When I finally made a desperate effort to try a few stuttering words in Spanish, my hosts winced in stifled pain. I shut up for the rest of the night.

Later, as Father Fred escorted me, a bewildered stranger, in the dark to the hut where I would live on the edge of the Colegio campus, a surly pack of Doberman pinschers and German shepherds growled, woofed, and sniffed at my legs. Father Fred said good-night. I was all alone in a large, barren, wood-walled room. Outside, the dogs barked, and, from somewhere beyond the school, the annoying thump-thump beat of some Peruvian popular song blared into the night.

My first night in Tacna I went to bed overwhelmed by a feeling of abandonment and depression—humiliated by my inability to understand or exchange an intelligible word of Spanish at dinner, committed, perhaps rashly, to work in a world radically different from anything I had ever known.

The next morning I was up at 5 A.M. for basketball practice at 5:30. There I stood dumbly by as my mentor, Bill McKeever, the volunteer I would replace, ran his ten shivering youths up and down the outdoor court.

After practice, back at the residence, I took a shower —or, more accurately, endured the inescapable pain of ice cold water battering my six foot, 180 pound trembling body.

Then I dried, dressed, and walked outside for my first undistracted look at where I was.

Somehow I had not noticed how dramatically the barbed wire fence separated our lovely property from the poor neighborhood almost in our back yard which, in my home town, would be considered a slum. A woman who had brought her plastic water bucket to an outdoor spigot suddenly straightened up, cocked her head, put her hands on her hips, and stared at me directly. Her children, in torn, dirty clothing, with dusty hands and feet, stared at me too—as my gold Seiko watch and gold college ring, in my imagination, took on enormous weight and proportion on my wrist and finger. Both were gifts; but the ring now became emblematic not so much of me as a person—as if Boston College had given me my identity—but of the world I had left behind.

For a passing second the woman's eyes and mine met. Perhaps she was as embarrassed as I.

III

Where I Come From

I grew up a conventional, faithful, but not remarkably pious Catholic—the first-born son, with a younger brother and sister—in a middle-class family in Meriden, Connecticut. My parents met in high school, married a few years later, and, within a few more years, were raising the three of us.

Educated in public schools, I seem to have had, from the beginning, a very lively imagination, which I fed for a while by reading library books—biographies of sports heroes, famous scientists and political leaders; then, for a while, by watching war movies on late afternoon TV as I dreamed of leading troops into battle; then, when I was a little more mature, by a TV advertisement called "Don't crawl under a rock." It was a call to join the Peace Corps, to "help others help themselves" in the "toughest job you'll ever love."

Sometimes, even though I was very young, I joined my politician grandfather on his campaign travels. While he worked most of his life making ball bearings in a General Motors factory, he was also an active member of the United Auto Workers Union and served sixteen years in the Connecticut State Senate and four years in the Connecticut House of Representatives. It meant something to all of us that he "knew the Kennedys." He would take me to the capital in Hartford, make his rounds, and introduce me to his friends and constituents. "You gotta be for the little guy," he told me again and again.

The Democrats, he said, were for the people, and the Republicans were against them. "It's that simple," he said, and I took his word for it.

If my political education was not very sophisticated, neither was my religious training. We went to catechism classes through eighth grade, but my parents did not attend mass often, and I don't remember ever saying grace before a meal.

My mother, who said she had stopped participating in the life of the church because it made her feel guilty all the time, continually warned me to beware of the Catholic "guilt complex." I remember getting the impression that it was hard to be good, that there were so many rules to follow and obstacles to overcome. If you ate thirty minutes before receiving communion it was a sin.

Swearing was a sin. If so, I've got a lot of sins. I still swear a lot. In eighth grade I said a bad word a week before confirmation; a friend heard me and threatened to tell a priest, and I was petrified lest I not be confirmed.

Gradually, however, the other Christianity made its way into my understanding. A young priest in our Holy Angels parish in South Meriden, Father Robert Lysz, talked of an all-forgiving, all-loving God. By explaining that Christianity was essentially about helping people, he motivated me to participate in service organizations. But it would be a long while before it dawned on me that Christ called us to a special association with poor.

Boston College, a sprawling university in the old, wealthy neighborhood of Chestnut Hill, just a few minutes west of downtown Boston, is—along with our long-time rival Holy Cross College in Worcester, Georgetown University in Washington, D.C., and Fairfield University in Connecticut—one of the better known of the twenty-eight American Jesuit colleges and universities.

Jesuit colleges have several characteristics in common: a reputation for high academic standards, though not necessarily for a highly developed intellectual life or a love of learning for its own sake; a warm, friendly-family, party atmosphere; a love of sports and beer cultivated early in high school, raised to a frenzy on St. Patrick's Day, and welding together generations of graduates by a common social bond; a "Jesuit tradition"—though many graduates never meet a Jesuit, and the nature of "Jesuit presence" is something on which not even all Jesuits would agree.

Meanwhile, Jesuit schools everywhere have, since Vatican II and a series of Jesuit General Congregations, defined themselves as committed to "faith and justice" as inseparable principles, and to developing their students as "men and women for others." As a result, although most graduates major in economics so they can go into business or compete to get into the top law and/or medical schools, a good number opt to live "for others" when they graduate. Some join a group called the Jesuit Volunteer Corps, a type of domestic Peace Corps which commits graduates for a year to social service projects in American inner cities, on Indian reservations or even in Alaska; or some become International Volunteers and undertake, under Jesuit auspices, Peace Corps-type projects in the third world.

Most of the time in our senior year, though, we went around laughing and joking as if every day was Saint Patrick's Day. After all, our quarterback was Doug Flutie, who won the Heisman Trophy in 1984 and got us into the Cotton Bowl in 1985. I lived with the same five guys for four years. The keg was always on tap.

My world, in a sense, was very small; and I loved it that way.

One roommate, Tony Smith, from Okemos, Michigan, used to break up parties with his Mick Jagger imitations. Tony, the resident philosopher, skeptic and social critic, pondered Madonna's impact on our culture, didn't like

Reagan, loved to make conservatives mad, and occasionally asked profound questions like, "What happens to your lap when you stand up?"

Mike Kuntz, from Allentown, Pennsylvania, said his goal in life was to make big money like his oilman father, who used to brag that he played football, both offense and defense, at Annapolis. But I think that if Mike did what he really wanted to do, he would have studied film at Columbia—because he and Tony used to sit around and talk about how they would shoot the opening scenes of the movies in their heads. Girls loved Mike, the most caring and generous guy in our group, with his curly hair and a perpetual tan from visiting his family's new Florida home. But they loved him as a friend, so he became the counselor to all our girlfriends.

Gonzalo Fernandez's parents—a doctor and a lawyer —were originally from Argentina and maintained a condo in Acapulco. The family was rich, so he spent a lot of money on clothes, played a lot of water polo, and drank a lot of beer. He was the mastermind of our social events, who turned our modular apartment—Mod 42B—into an entertainment center on weekend nights.

His sidekick Jay Greely and he chased a lot of women and raised a lot of hell. In freshman year they bet on a game one time where the loser had to go down to the second floor in the girl's dorm and "flash" this girl named Suzie who, we thought, was a real pain.

The sixth member of our apartment team was Paul Connors, the fifth of nine children, the captain of the soccer team, with a good sense of humor and a very relaxed attitude toward study. He did study hard, but didn't get up-tight about grades. My favorite Paul Connors story is about the time he fell asleep at the end of one of our beer-guzzling evenings and we carried him on his mattress out to the 50-yard line of Alumni Stadium. We were going to leave him there, but the police made us bring him home.

Much as I loved these friends, during the week I often saw them no more than an hour or so a day—that time around midnight when I would wind down drinking beer with them after pouring my daytime energies (9 A.M. to 7 P.M.) into class and student government and my evening energy (8 P.M. to after 11 P.M.) into my books. In fact, thinking about, planning for and worrying over the details of UGBC (Undergraduate Government of Boston College) virtually defined me as a person—except for those weekend nights when I just let go and became one, big, happy drunk, dancing and laughing with whoever came along.

But in senior year the most important visitor to our Mod 42B on B.C.'s lower campus and member of "the group" for me became Jill Alper. She was (and still is) pretty, smiling, caring, supportive and, like me, ambitious both for me and for herself. She helped me with my speeches, shared her insights into people, and in time replaced Paul as the person with whom I would talk out my frustrations, my political and personal problems. By the time graduation approached we were in love.

Meanwhile, our dreamworld—as if we were all characters in an MGM technicolor musical about college—went on. We had no debts and paid no taxes, we lived from moment to moment. One afternoon a high school student campus tour group passed Tony and me and Tony blurted out (though not really loud enough to be heard), "Don't come here! You'll have a great time, and when it's all over they'll just kick you out, back into the streets."

Of course we also dreamed of the future and argued politics, philosophy and religion, but our main concern in life was really just us.

Or so it seemed. In spite of my surface obsession with my tight clique of friends and my political ambitions, some psychological and moral seeds planted by those childhood TV war movies, in which I had imagined myself the hero, and the practical helping-people Christianity of Father Lysz had been germinating. Everyone assumed I would go

21

to law school, but I had been thinking of doing something different with my life for a while. I had been exploring the idea of going abroad, working with the poor.

I'm afraid it came as no surprise that when I told my family and Jill that I had decided to put off law school and go to Peru, they were against it.

Jill wanted me to be around.

I told her two years would go by quickly. It would be a time for both of us to grow, I said—although this line of reasoning hardly made her happy.

When I called home with the news, my father said I was wasting my time: "None of those programs help the poor," he said. "They never do any good. They never make any change. Most people who work in these programs come out frustrated. Your father has a lot of experience with a lot of different people. I know what I'm talking about."

He always referred to himself as "your father" when he was trying to prove his point.

My father's family had been on welfare from the time he was four until he was eighteen. But he struggled. He worked for the Firestone Tire and Rubber Company; in 1978 he opened his own car repair and tire sales business. He achieved those basic satisfactions which to his peers and his value system signified the good life: a wife whom he himself had crowned as high school prom queen, a good house in a nice neighborhood, three children, summer vacations and a dog. He did not want his son to throw all this away.

"Why don't you just be a lawyer?" he said. "Take care of yourself first, then take care of others." After all, that's what most of my fellow graduates were doing.

But somehow, in some of the Sunday night masses at B.C., particularly those where a young Jesuit, Julio Giulietti, spoke, I picked up the idea that I should be doing something different—that those childhood fantasies of

"Called"

22

being a sports hero or war hero could still be acted out, only now in service of the poor. Julio was the director of a relatively new program—a variation on the Jesuit Volunteer Corps and the Peace Corps—called the Boston College International Volunteer Program, that gives young men and women like me a chance to test our ideals by putting them to work.

Toward the end of the year, Julio sat down with my parents and, thanks to his diplomatic skills, they gave their consent for me to work in Tacna for two years.

In reality, they had little choice. I was twenty-two and determined to make my own decision.

One night in June, a few days after I had returned from our post-graduation sail in the Virgin Islands with Mike, Tony, Gonz, Jay and Paul, I called my parents to tell them about the trip. My mother was stuttering a bit on the phone: "So, Jeff, um . . . has your father or anyone said anything to you yet?"

"About what, Ma? What's going on?"

"Well, you know, your father and I have had a rough year, you know."

My heart started to beat fast. I was in my room alone and hoped that no one walked in.

Finally, my father got on the line and blurted: "Your mother and I are going to live apart for a while. We're going to a counselor to figure out how to divide things up in case that's necessary."

My mother came on the phone again to help explain that they had tried to make a go of it and that it just hadn't worked; she planned to leave our home at the end of the summer and move into a condominium where she hoped to begin a new life.

My sister Debra called later to tell me that my parents had not been happy together for a long time and that their separation was for the best.

For the best? How could the break-up of my family be

"for the best"? I was completely stunned. The fact that I, unlike my sister, had not seen it coming, that I had failed to perceive—probably because I had been so absorbed with my politics and my substitute family of roommates—how my parents related to one another, raised questions about my own maturity, my own ability to assess reality.

Yet I had not been completely blind. They would snap at and bad-mouth one another; but when the three of us returned from school—Deb from Roger Williams College in Rhode Island and Greg from Springfield College in Massachusetts where he studied physical therapy—they tried to cover it up.

One time when we all went to New York right after Christmas in 1984, after Greg and Deb and I had spent most of our time in our room talking about mom and dad, I confronted my mother point blank and asked if she and dad were getting a divorce, and she said, "No, we're not getting a divorce. We're going through a tough time, but we'll get through it. Neither of us wants to get divorced."

So I kept telling myself and the others—and Jill, whose parents also were separating—that things would work out.

I was kidding myself. Every time we were together things were worse. Even at graduation, when they did their best to put on a good front, they had a little tiff in the parking lot on the way to the car.

So when the facts finally sank in, I called Jill and she came over and I told her and she cried. I had not yet learned to cry when I should, so she cried for both of us.

My grandfather said to put it behind me, that it was their problem, not mine. He was right in that there was now nothing I could do; but in another way he was wrong: it was still my problem. On the one hand I had the fact, which I cannot emphasize too strongly, that I had been raised in a very strong and supportive family, with all the benefits of encouragement, family vacations and college education to which the middle class aspire. But it also meant that my perfect little world was now in pieces.

When I left Jill to go to Peru in early October, I cried like a baby all the way from Boston to Connecticut. When I left Miami for Lima after spending my last four days in the United States with my grandparents, I could see my grandfather holding back the tears as he hugged me, lowered his head and turned away. My grandmother was already in tears. As they left I closed the door and wept and wept as I had never done before.

IV

The Once-Golden Kingdom

By almost any standard of measurement, Peru—though wealthy in its Inca history and spectacularly beautiful in its Andes mountain scenery—is one of the most godforsaken countries in the world.

The population of over twenty million—a collection of ethnically diverse groups, with those of Spanish and mixed blood (mestizos) controlling the wealth and living mainly along the coast, and the Indians (half the population) living in extreme poverty in the mountains and coastal cities—has been facing a triple crisis for the last decade: economic chaos, drugs and civil war.

Strikes, poverty, unemployment, food shortages and an astronomical inflation rate characterized the economic crisis. The illegal cocaine traffic enables Peru to supply sixty-five percent of the cocaine that ends up in American cities; in my first year alone, Peru exported about 64,000 tons of coca paste. In fact, coca is Peru's largest export, earning more than one billion dollars a year, and its production employs as many as a million people in the trade.

In the escalating, frustrating civil war, the principal foe was—and remains—the cold-blooded Maoist guerrilla army of an estimated two to five thousand youths called Sendero Luminoso, the Shining Path.

Their movement took seed among philosophy students at the University of Ayacucho in the 1960s, apparently filling a moral and intellectual void which the traditional value systems, including that put forward by the church, failed to fill. They offer no clear political or economic alternatives to established political parties.

But the established parties have governed so incompetently and so corruptly that the people have become vulnerable to the message of almost anyone who promises something fresh and new. For example, shortly before I arrived, the social democratic APRA (the American Popular Revolutionary Alliance, founded in 1924 in Mexico City and called the Apristas) had returned to power under the leadership of Alan Garcia, a young, charismatic—but emotionally unpredictable—anti-American who presented himself as a new spokesman for the third world.

But already he was beginning to fade and rumors often spread of an impending military coup, as if only the old officer class, called militares, the hereditary army leaders, could save the country from anarchy.

In this atmosphere, the Shining Path simply spread terror, with the expectation that the annihilation of the present state will lead to a Maoist-communist utopia. In exercises of violence that border on ritual, the Senderistas enter little towns, gather together the local governor, the mayor, the justice of the peace and the frightened townspeople in the town square, conduct a mock public trial, harangue their audience about government corruption, and execute the peasants' leaders before their eyes. They also enjoy cutting out their victims' eyes and tongues and slicing off their sexual organs. In this way, and in the government's attempt to track them down, an estimated twenty thousand people, of which many have been killed by paramilitary death squads, have met death since 1980.

According to Tina Rosenberg in the *New Republic* (January 18, 1990), "since 1987 Peruvian security forces have 'disappeared' more people than any other in the world. From 1982 to 1986, more than 6,000 people were killed in the state of Ayacucho alone, the vast majority of them unarmed civilians." Therefore, as a result of government oppression, the Sendero movement is growing. And promises from politicians that a get-tough policy will solve the problem are suspect.

Most of the Sendero effort is centered in the province of Huancayo, to the east of Lima and Lima's breadbasket, where they bombed a parish led by a Chicago Jesuit because he was running a training center for peasants. Some of this activity has taken place around Puno, on Lake Titicaca, about one hundred and fifty miles to the northeast of Tacna—close enough for the social and political problems of Puno, including their periodic drought and flooding, to impinge on us, as part of their population, both frightened by the war and drawn by the contraband traffic with Chile, shifted in our direction. In rural Puno, according to Tina Rosenberg in the *New Republic* (October 9, 1989), one in seven families has electricity, only forty percent of the population have access to schools, and there is one doctor for every twenty-five thousand people. I would too soon see the consequences of this last detail.

First we had to see Lima, where all the country's problems parade themselves on a larger scale.

In *The Old Patagonian Express*, the story of Paul Theroux's 1977 train trip through Latin America, he describes Peru as "once a golden kingdom occupying a third of the continent," now the victim of a "mighty tumble." Lima, he says, has "the look of Rangoon, the same heat, and colonial relics and corpse odors." It is like "a violated tomb in which only the sorry mummy of withered nationalism is left."

After two weeks at Tacna, Bonnie, Leigh, and I took a twenty-nine hour bus ride up the coast to Lima for a month of language study at an Augustinian retreat house. We had looked forward to the change of scene, but the overall effect of the month in this dismal and lawless city was to aggravate and deepen the intense spells of loneliness and depression that had begun to hit me the first day I arrived.

The streets of Lima were filled with noise, noise, noise—half-wrecked cars belching their exhaust into the already poisonous air; pushcart vendors yelling, "Oye, gringo, buy my apples! Buy my olives! Buy my potatoes!" Everyone shouting, pushing, trying to survive.

The behavior of Peruvian men disgusted us. Men in business suits urinated in the streets. Married men we knew abused their wives and carried on extramarital affairs as if infidelity was accepted practice. Several times married men even called up Bonnie and Leigh to ask them out. Often we were too revolted by everything we saw to even attempt to understand the society we were part of.

But I made an effort to mix with the workers at the retreat house where we lived and with their neighborhood friends. At their house parties the men would pass a bottle around the room, where each person would pour a little in a common cup, drink, and pass the cup and bottle to the next person in line. Swigging liquor from the same cup with twenty other men put me off a bit, but I got used to it. Once they had a few drinks they peppered the American with questions: Does everyone in America get as much sex as they do in the movies? How powerful is the Ku Klux Klan? Is it true that the CIA killed Kennedy because he wanted to help the poor?

But I often found their questions a nuisance. The grimness and violence of the city were worsening the depression that was already wearing me out.

A heavy, damp, gray cloud cover loomed perpetually over the urban landscape, but no rain fell to relieve the gloom or wash the reeking garbage and human excrement from the streets.

On these streets—where thieves snatched visitors' cameras, bags, watches, neck chains and even eyeglasses—we never felt secure. Poor men, women and children groped at us pleading for money and food. The Indian children—of indeterminate age, very short and dark, with round, almost oriental faces, high cheekbones, and

29

narrow, fierce eyes—would stare in my eyes, then gesture with their fingers toward their mouths, as if to say they were starving and only I could feed them.

Like most travelers in Peru, we escaped the tortures of Lima for a two-week trip south to Cuzco, the ancient Inca capital high in the Andes, and the spectacular Sacred Valley watered by the Urubamba River to its north; and then we journeyed farther south to Puno and Arequipa for a better understanding of the larger section of southern Peru of which Tacna was a part.

Puno is a university town—eight thousand of its eighty thousand inhabitants are students—on the shore of Lake Titicaca. Arequipa, with its population of about 850,000, lies in a valley at the foot of a snow-capped volcano and is the commercial center of the south. But the city that visitors to Peru remember most is Cuzco.

Cuzco's altitude, over ten thousand feet, forces its new visitors to slow down and catch their breath, to eat lightly and drink less—at least on the first day. It ruled the Inca empire, which stretched from Ecuador to Chile and was held together by a common religion, sun worship, and a rigorously planned economy, from the eleventh century until it was conquered by the Spaniards in the sixteenth century.

Viewed from its surrounding mountainsides, where tourists and travelers scramble among a series of Inca ruins and photograph domesticated llamas—once they have tipped their owners—with the spires of its seventeenth century cathedral dominating its Plaza de Armas, Cuzco is one of the loveliest cities I have ever seen. Though its population of over 200,000 are mostly Indians, and its main attraction is supposed to be the ancient Inca walls which constitute the masonry of many mid-city buildings, we enjoyed it for its international flavor and its lively night life. In three years I came here five times.

I'm afraid I'm not much of an historian, nor a poet. So the mysteries of ancient Peru buried or half-revealed within the massive walls of Sacsayhuaman, the sun temple a half hour above Cuzco, or the fortress of Ollaytantambo overlooking the Urubamba, or the glorious mountain-top ruins of Machu Picchu, which leave most travelers—including Paul Theroux—both breathless and speechless, will not shed their mysteriousness in these pages.

But in spite of the several times I either took the bus up Machu Picchu's perilous winding dirt road or climbed the dangerous ledge path up the side of the taller Hyuana Picchu, which overlooks the ruins of the "lost city," each trip was a new thrill.

Before, the trip to Machu Picchu had been a travel poster, or a picture in a high school geography book. I had read that it was the greatest ruin in the western world. Now this sacred site, which had been hidden from ancient and modern invaders until 1911, was part of my experience, my spiritual life.

V

A Death in the Family

We returned to Tacna in mid-December where the approach of Christmas, rather than perk us up with some of its traditional joy, added to our distress and homesickness. Father Fred, whom I was getting to know better with each day, did his best to bring us back to life. As a leader, dapper and well dressed, he exuded a quiet, unsmiling manliness which some older friends compared to that of the actors Alan Ladd or Henry Fonda and which we compared to Clint Eastwood. In a lot of ways he had the wisdom of both my father and my grandfather and replaced both of them for me in Peru. He took us to the beach on Christmas Day, where he ran along the water's edge and gave us a laugh by standing on his head, then treated us to dinner. But our thoughts were three thousand miles away with our families and old friends.

As work began at Cristo Rey, I drifted away from Bonnie and Leigh. It's a fact of volunteer life, both in the United States and overseas, that young men and women thrown together in a strange situation often fail to establish warm and supportive communities. Each member has problems of loneliness and frustration that he or she tries to sort out alone. Bonnie and Leigh didn't have the freedom they were used to and were frustrated by the machismo culture. I missed my apartment pals from B.C. and was embarrassed by my still poor Spanish.

Although we shared a common cooking area, Bonnie and Leigh didn't see much value in common meals; so, for my entire first year in Peru, until Father Fred invited me to eat with the school community, I cooked and ate alone.

I tried writing more letters to friends and almost-friends at home; then I grew resentful when they didn't write back.

Meanwhile, my clumsiness with the language was still making me look silly in front of the boys. Stumbling around the basketball court with my team one day I told them my favorite player was Boston Celtics star Larry Bird.

Bird in Spanish, they said, smiling, is "pajaro." "You're Larry Pajaro." More smiles.

"Show us how Pajaro does it," they said.

I moved toward the basket and tried a tricky layup that miraculously went in. "I'm Larry Pajaro. That's who I am," I said as I tried to imitate him with shot after shot.

"Way to go, Pajaro! Do it again, Pajaro!" the kids shouted.

Pajaro became my nickname. They called out "Pajaro" when I missed a shot in a game or even when they passed me on campus. I wrote in my diary that this was a sign I was popular with the kids.

I mentioned to Father Fred that the kids called me "Pajaro."

"Is that right?" he said with a straight face—although his lips curled just slightly.

Then Bill told me; he had to blurt it out: "Here 'pajaro' is slang for penis. They're calling you penis."

This was not a good start.

In February, the height of the Peruvian summer, the pace of life picked up for all of us during Cristo Rey's social service month. In its attempt to form students as "men and women for others"—a phrase propagated by the previous Jesuit superior general Pedro Arrupe—Father Fred had developed a complex program to "teach justice" to the student body.

33

A basic ingredient of the plan was the makeup of the student body—sixty percent of whom come from middle and upper class families and forty percent from the poor. The hope was that their interaction would help mitigate the class-conscious value systems of the richer boys. The next step included an academic analysis of the evils and injustices in Peruvian society; then there would be regular liturgies, with the hope that the gospel message would reinforce the social analysis. Finally, our get-your-hands-dirty project: twenty-two adolescents, two faculty, one priest, Ricardo Gonzalez, S.J., and I were to spend a month two hours away, in the sweltering, coastal farming community of Ite (population six hundred), building a kindergarten classroom for the public school.

Ite looks out from the hillside to the Pacific Ocean, where no one can fish or swim, its shore stained a dirty green from the pollutants spewed out by the Southern Peru Copper Corporation. The pollution, the villagers told me, was the fault of "bad gringos." The farmers produce milk, peppers and fruit. There is no electricity, one phone line to Tacna, and one fly-infested, seatless toilet located near where we worked and ate—and where I sat and expelled my meals as soon as I ingested them in several days of debilitating diarrhea.

Divided into construction teams, directed by an Aymara Indian foreman, Marcelino Capacuti, under the baking sun we shoveled dirt and sand, mixed cement, loaded rocks into wheelbarrows, laid a foundation, and poured cement columns and beams. I knew little of the process or the Spanish words for the tools, but I learned. My other jobs, besides working alongside our boys, were to wake them in the morning and play soccer with them after work.

Each day, when work was over, I stripped down to shorts and sandals, soaped up my body and poured cold water over myself for a nightly shower—as small children, teenage girls and townspeople stood around and laughed at the sight of my white flesh.

Suddenly one morning in late January as I was sitting in the local store—my sense of isolation to some degree broken and a separate peace half-achieved—a police officer brought news from the outside world.

"I'm sorry to hear what happened in your country," the officer said.

"What happened?" I asked, with no idea what he was referring to.

"Challenger . . . kabloom!" he said, clapping his hands together.

Kabloom. What all Americans knew in an instant, and indeed watched repeatedly on their TV screens in the minutes and hours after it happened, took days to spread by word of mouth through our little community. And here they gossiped about it with special interest because I— their American—was there; the death of the astronauts became a death in their family as well.

In spite of the cultural distance, I was achieving some moments of at-home-ness with these townspeople, especially during carnival—their Mardi Gras—when I drank and danced with them in the plaza on Sundays. Some thought I was a priest and asked my blessing (which I once gave to two drunks) and many asked the usual questions about the United States, where, they assumed, everyone was rich.

Meanwhile, my relationship with the boys, which had gone fairly smoothly when I worked alongside them, turned into a war. When the teacher in charge of discipline went home after ten days, I was put in charge. When construction lagged because of shortages, I tried to compensate by making them work harder. The upper middle class students among them, who were used to servants doing their manual work for them at home, resisted all the more.

With my authority compromised by my ignorance of both building techniques and colloquial Spanish, I fell back on my short temper and foul mouth. When one dark-skinned fifteen year old refused to move some bags of cement, I called him, in English, a "stupid shit," and his friends picked up the insult in a chant, "Stupid shit black," thus humiliating both him and me.

When they refused to turn out their lights and go to bed at 10 P.M., I personally snuffed out their candles. When a fifteen year old swore at me in the dark, I loomed over his cot in a rage and shone my flashlight in his face. Not knowing what to do next I just kept the light on him— as a punishment. Then the batteries died, leaving me humiliated, a laughing-stock, in the dark.

One Monday afternoon, Fernando, a tall, lanky basketball player who used to enjoy asking me about the soft-core American porn movies popular in Peru, returned to Ite after some days back in Tacna because of illness. He had also been one of the ringleaders in the "Larry Pajaro" gag.

"Hey Larry!" he called.

I blew up. I had had it with these kids. Stupidly, I hit him. He fell back, stunned.

As I walked away trembling, I heard the kids chant in unison: "Hey, Larry! Hey, Larry! Hey, Larry!"

When I tried to send him home, the whole gang turned against me, pouring out their grievances at a public meeting: I swore and yelled at them, woke them up roughly, pulling off the covers, didn't understand them, and worked them too hard.

They were right. Besides, there are few forces as uncontrollable and devastating as an aggrieved group of teenagers who have gotten an adult's ear.

Ricardo Gonzalez, the jovial Jesuit priest in charge, who tried to be friends with everybody, puffed his ciga-

Top: Jeff Thielman with children of the Pueblo Joven in Tacna. **Bottom:** Children from Pueblo Joven attending mass at the Cristo Rey Center for the Working Child. The celebrant is Father John Foley, S.J., from Chicago, director of the Collegio Cristo Rey.

rettes and nervously explained to me that Fernando would have to stay. We made peace, and in the last ten days I regained a measure of respect.

Some of this, as I look back on it, is silly, and much of it is very painful. But it is nothing compared to what I saw on Saturday, February 8.

We were all very tired, so a friendly farmer had agreed to drive us—the boys, Ricardo, two nurses and myself—to the beach for the afternoon. It was about four in the afternoon when we returned, and waiting for us in front of the health station near our rooms was a skinny, cross-eyed farmer, a "campesino." Tired and worn, his head bowed, he had been waiting four hours. He said that his name was Sebastian and that he was twenty-two years old.

He and his wife Herenia (nineteen) had moved to Ite from Puno to escape floods and a food shortage and had set themselves up in a hut only a fifteen minute walk away, working a patron's land for fourteen intis (eighty cents) a day. They had a one year old child.

That morning, around three A.M., another child had been born. By eleven it had died.

Rosa, the nurse, questioned him, while the wife of the farmer who had driven us to the beach, who had been listening from the cabin of their truck, let out a sigh. Why had they not come for help when she went into labor? He stood silent, head hanging; the farmer's wife drove away. While Rosa prepared the paperwork, Ricardo sprayed him with more questions. Was the child baptized? He began to sob softly.

Together our group, which now included a policeman, made its way down the hill on foot to Sebastian's house.

The tiny, one-room, thatch-roofed, dirt-floored, windowless, adobe hut, provided by the patron, smelled of the cow manure they used for cooking fuel. What should have been a reverent silence was broken by the incessant buzzing of a swarm of flies. On the shelf lay a dirty razor blade which Sebastian had used to cut the baby's umbilical cord.

Herenia lay in a small bed. On the edge of the bed, wrapped in filthy rags, was the dead child.

Rosa unwrapped it, exposing the tiny, slightly-swollen corpse with a belly button bloodied from the razor's cut. As she laid it for a moment on the table, the flies landed on the dead child and crawled all over its eyes in a way that, for a minute, made it look as if they were opening and shutting, mockingly blinking at us all.

I stared and stared at the dead child, and my mind and body went numb. I was twenty-three and I had never before seen a corpse that wasn't in a coffin. I had read that every six minutes an infant under one year old dies in Peru. At Boston College we had fasted and prayed about world hunger. But never in my wildest imagination did I dream I would ever see anything as bad as this.

I came from a powerful, "anything is possible" country, and in this hut in Ite, Peru, I was helpless. All I could do was pray for the child, for the family, and for my own self-control.

The police officer and nurse examined the child and matter-of-factly determined that it had died of natural causes. We returned the fly-covered corpse to the table, Father Ricardo said a prayer over it, and we left.

The next day, Sunday, Ricardo, Rosa, Sebastian and his friends and I buried the child in a cardboard milk carton labeled "Leche Gloria" in a sandy grave under some stones and a cross of sticks. Then, true to the funeral customs of the Peruvian poor, Sebastian passed around a bottle of coke and a single glass.

The child never had a name and I do not know to this day whether it was a boy or a girl.

Rosa told me later that the baby had been born six weeks premature, that the mother did not want another child because they could never feed it on fourteen intis a day, and that she had tried to kill it by regularly beating her womb.

The patrons, of course—those who had been born on the lucky side of Latin American history—could drive their wives in labor to a hospital, one hour away in Ilo. The more I observed and the more I listened, the more obsessed I became with what I had seen at Ite. We returned to Tacna leaving the schoolroom roofless; the materials had never arrived. I couldn't get that child's unnecessary death off my mind. And I vowed to do something to avenge what I saw in that hut.

VI

"When I Was Your Age . . ."

For the next month, before school reopened in April, determined to shake that town up, I tried to run a one-man war against those ultimately responsible for Sebastian's and Herenia's poverty and the child's death—the landowners who paid Sebastian fourteen intis a day when the minimum wage was twenty-three intis.

In Tacna I rode my bike over to the Office of the Labor Ministry, where I confronted the head of Employment and Social Security, Oscar Galdos, with my story. The little gray-haired man looked up from the newspaper open on his desk; behind him, on the wall, was a sign: "Debureaucratization is the responsibility of all Peruvians."

"That's terrible, just terrible," he replied. "It even makes me ashamed." He looked up, half-amused, half-irritated, by the idealistic young gringo towering over his desk. "But we have so many problems in this country."

Problems, problems.

Their office, he explained, could not investigate until a worker complained; a worker could not afford the two-hour trip from Ite to Tacna to file the complaint. And if he does complain he is often fired. So . . . what can anyone do?

"So many problems. What we need is an 'hombre fuerte' (strong man) who will come along and change everything."

He smiled at me: "You know, when I was your age, I wanted to change things too . . ."

What a loser, I thought. The man has led a wasted life, and he's trying to justify it.

For the next six weeks I spent every day in pursuit of some government official, determined to crack this system. Each one put me off, failed to show up, didn't return my call, couldn't get a car, was off to a meeting or celebrating a birthday. When the mayor of Ite visited Tacna in June, I gave him one hundred copies of the minimum wage law, and he said he would distribute them. But in the end I felt like a fool. These people were lazy time-servers stringing a kid along, convinced I'd just fade away if they kept patting me on the head.

This was a land of too damn many tomorrows. I was batting my head against the legacy of hundreds of years of Spanish colonial rule, when the royal representative had used a multitude of scribes, lawyers, and notaries not to serve the people but to control the empire. After the nineteenth century revolutions the bureaucracy had hung on —manifesting itself in a complex system of sloth and favoritism—in the self-perpetuating Peruvian fatalism: since nothing works, why try to make it work?

Father Fred had told me I'd be wasting my time, but that if I wanted to try to force some changes here, I might learn something.

I did.

VII

Why Am I Here?

The simplest, most honest thing to say about my teaching in my first year is that, although I improved the boys' writing, my teaching was bad. In my classes in history and religion, at the beginning I understood about half of what the boys said, and in my small English class we often just wasted time talking in Spanish until Father Fred came by and caught us.

My initial dreams about being a great teacher paralleled my childhood TV-movie fantasies of being a war hero, but, in reality, my classes were a wacky mix of laughter and terror. Laughter when sometimes I myself would break up at the sight of a silly expression on a fat kid's face and the class would erupt a second later, or when I would stumble into another of my language gaffes—like the time I warned them, "If I see one of you moving your eyes, I'll assume you are plagiarizing," but, instead of "plagiar," I said "pajear," to masturbate.

Terror in that I used my tough standards to punish the students when they rebelled. I delighted in giving someone a zero for cheating—my only revenge for the string of humiliations they inflicted. They told me to my face I was "boring." They refused to call me by the proper title, "professor," and threw papers at me when I turned my back. With smirks on their little faces, they baited me with questions they knew I couldn't answer—"Tell us, which were the busiest Latin American port cities during the

colonial era?'' In my daily tirades, I screamed "Never"—
as in "Never talk when the teacher is talking"—so often
that they changed my name to "Nunca" (Never) and
yelled "Hey Nunca!" in the lunch room or in gym class or
wherever I appeared.

At least they weren't still calling me Penis.

Basketball coaching went equally well—which is to
say, disastrously. When I was growing up in Meriden I had
been cut from four baseball teams; and in high school,
when the soccer coach played me a total of ten minutes in
twelve games and I decided to hand in my jersey, the
coach put it bluntly: "You lack a lot of skills with the ball,
you're also pretty slow, and you're a bit uncoordinated. It
would take you a lot of time to be a halfway decent
player."

At the end of the school year I quit coaching. I had yet
to find something I did well. What was I doing here?

I began to find at least part of the answer in Jesus—
Jesus Paz, one of the Cristo Rey poor students, who had
stopped coming to class and whom I sought out in his miserable pueblo joven straw shack. His father had abandoned him, his five brothers, and his mother for another
woman years before; his mother, who had moved in with
another man, had no room for him in their hut, and he was
left alone in this hovel, studying by candlelight or in the
early dawn. When he saw me he put his head down and
said he was too ashamed to come to school.

Working with Jesus, trying to find him a home, I got
the first inklings of the satisfaction denied me in the
classroom. I was helping someone who was poor.

One day in March, when I was still biking into town in
my fruitless effort to pressure the bureaucracy to enforce
the minimum wage in Ite, for fun I started joking around
—quibbling over prices—with a bunch of shoeshine boys.

Most were barefoot. A few wore black sandals made

of tire rubber. Each carried a box with shoe polish, brushes and rags. Some looked as young as six or seven; the oldest, fifteen. They had tough looks, but were eager to make a sale, especially to the white-skinned "gringo" who would surely pay more than a local.

"Hey, mister, where are you from? Estados Unidos?"

"Yes."

"What's it like over there?"

I tried to say it was big and beautiful, but I changed the subject. "Where do you boys live?"

"Over there."

"How much do you make shining shoes?"

No answer. I was disappointed. No conversation developed. I mounted my bike to ride on. But one shouted, "Hey, mister, what's your name?"

"Jeff."

"Yef?"

"Jeff."

"Will we see you again?"

"Yes."

Along with their pals, who sold papers, washed cars, or simply stole for a living, they were the resourceful children of hundreds of thousands of Aymara Indians who, for over three generations, have poured from the Andes into the cities in search of, first, survival, and then a better life. Desperate for even a little money to hold their lives together, they send their sons, some as young as six or seven, into the streets to hustle.

In the barber shop, where the owner had chased the kids away when I came in, the patrons and the barber groused and groaned about them in a dialogue anyone could probably have heard in Meriden, or Boston, or any American town.

"These kids are trouble. You've got to watch 'em. They're always stealing candy and soda pop from the street vendors."

"They come from Puno with their families. Damned

Damned Indians

Indians! They take our water, make money in contraband . . ."

"They breed like dogs. . . . This used to be a nice
quiet place to live."

These boys—and the standard middle and upper class
reaction to them—were my introduction to that scandal-
ous cultural phenomenon that confuses and shocks any
alert traveler—at least those who have not, in their roles
as plastic-coated tourists, sealed themselves off from everything unpleasant the streets and countrysides throw at
them: the failure of the so-called advanced civilizations to
care for their poor.

Confronted, as he passed through Bogotá, with beggars—"blind, lame, palsied; children, women, old men,
infants—naked in the cold—being dandled on the knees
of cringing hags"—Paul Theroux wrote: "To remark on
the number of beggars is perhaps to make an observation
of no great insight, like saying it is a continent of soldiers
and shoeshine boys. . . . But why, I wondered, were so
many of them children? Not sick or lame, and not carrying
signs, they lived among the ruined buildings and ran in
packs through the streets. They were lively, but they lived
like rats. . . . It does not occur to the wealthy Colombian
that these urchins are anything but vermin—and why
house them or feed them when it is so much cheaper to put
up a high fence around the house to keep them out?"

So I stopped and joked with the boys with the torn
clothes and dirty, polish-stained hands again on the way
out. Then, as the weeks went by, I managed to stop in on
them again and again. My mind was racing ahead. Somehow these kids, in a way that was not yet clear to me, fit
into the larger scheme of my coming to Peru.

I convinced my students to make these boys their required service project and invited the street kids for a
Saturday morning of soccer with my mostly middle class
students on the fields of Cristo Rey.

46

At first it flopped—because the street kids didn't believe me when I told them our bus would pick them up. But soon it worked. They came. They ran and screamed and tumbled on the rich, green turf. We picked up thirty of them downtown in the bus, played for hours in the hot sun, gave them sandwiches and soda and sent them home. Each Saturday morning they kept coming.

This was just the beginning. They needed a real program. The social worker assigned by the city, Bertha Vargas, had organized three hundred shoeshine boys into a union; but that's all she had done. They needed sports. A club. A center. A place that would, at least once a week, give them a safe and trusting world, a peek at some alternative to the cut-throat, aimless existence that consumed them. I talked to the mayor, to businessmen. These kids needed arts and crafts. They needed someone who cared what happened to their lives. They needed me.

So far I had been begging money for soda and sandwiches from students' parents; now I started a little serious fund-raising, a letter to seventy friends and friends of friends back home with the story of what had happened at Ite and my hopes for a center. On June 16, 1986, a businessman, Miguel Garcia, the father of one of my students, called and offered us a small abandoned building he owned near the center of town on Avenida Bolognesi, with water and electricity, free for two years. It needed a lot of work to get it in shape, but we took it.

Scraping together all the cash we had, $85, we sent out our old friend Capacuti, the custodian of the auditorium at Cristo Rey and our construction partner from our social project at Ite, and who had done some smuggling in his past, to buy the first basic item we needed to make the center a decent place. We don't know where he got it, and I never saw a receipt, but he returned with the cheapest toilet he could find.

We were on our way.

47

VIII

Maybe I Am Going Nuts

Support at school unfortunately was melting. The students griped about playing soccer with the street kids because the street kids—true to form—played rough. My new project made me miss teachers' meetings, and a few times I was late for class.

Father Ricardo, my immediate supervisor, the chubby negotiator during my squabble with the rebellious students at Ite, had confronted me in the Jesuit kitchen with words I was not ready to hear: "You should know, Jeff, that most of those kids come just for the food. They pass the word to their friends that there's soda and sandwiches. I know. We did the same thing in Lima, and they came just for the food. . . . And I don't think it's fair to trick our parents, taking their money and making them believe some great transformation is taking place on Saturday mornings. Don't fool yourself, either."

I was furious. What had this clown ever done for the poor?

Nevertheless, on Monday, June 30, Capacuti and another worker started the renovations. From 5 A.M. till 6:30 A.M. I went through the motions of being a basketball coach, standing around thinking about myself while Oscar Quelopana, another staff member, ran the team through drills; then I zipped down to the construction site to check on materials, where I paced around our thirty-three by five meter lot and worried about myself some more.

I was deep into a challenging project which absorbed my energies, but I could not shake home out of my mind. All I could think of was that my parents were splitting. My father had visited for a week in March, and we traveled and lived like tourists and, insofar as we could, we came to terms with the separation that had become a divorce. "It's the best thing," he said.

In a terrible irony, part of the problem in their marriage had been that it was too centered on the family; and when first I, and then my sister Deb and my brother Greg went away to college, they were left alone at 19 Jepson Lane. But they had married so young, and had children so quickly—"You just got married and had kids in those days," my mother told me—that it was twenty-five years before they discovered that they didn't like being together.

Jill, whom I had dated for nearly a year, phoned once a month or so but seldom wrote. Yet she filled up my fantasy life just about every day. She had promised to visit in August. Most of my social life involved drinking beer on Friday nights with the Cristo Rey male faculty. I had tried two dates with a slightly older school teacher, but her parents always wanted her home by 11 P.M.

Then in mid-June, both the political situation and my personal life got worse.

The government quashed a Shining Path prison rebellion by ordering the army to massacre the prisoners, many of whom had raised their hands in surrender. Soon after, a hitherto inviolate, renowned tourist train, which daily carries hundreds of people from all over the world from Cuzco to the "lost city" of Machu Picchu, was blown up or derailed. The violence was attributed to the Shining Path and made headlines everywhere. The United States State Department issued travelers' warnings, and word of mouth began to spread that Peru was too dangerous to visit.

49

My mother and grandmother ignored the warnings and came, as scheduled, for ten days in July.

Jill did not.

In spite of a week of phone calls on my part—for which she paid—in which I pleaded with her, tried to convince her that the American press had exaggerated the danger, she caved in to family pressure, to her father's opposition, and cancelled the trip.

The moment I put down the phone was a terrible moment in which all the loneliness, depression, and self-doubt that had threatened to cripple me since I had arrived, but which I had temporarily fought off by plunging into some new activity, came to a head. A while back, in my anger and self pity, I had nicknamed her "la muerta," "the dead one," because she had so rarely written or called. "F--k this," I shouted out loud to an empty room as I slammed the receiver down. "I don't need this shit!"

In Peru winter comes in July. But since no houses in Tacna or cities like it have indoor central heating, we survived the cold nights, as the cold winter wind swept through our wooden-walled rooms, with kerosene heaters, and we bundled up in thermal underwear, sweatsuits, socks and hoods. That night, July 3, 1986, doubly distracted by the knowledge that back home America, with fireworks and TV spectaculars, was on the eve of celebrating the one hundredth anniversary of the Statue of Liberty, I trudged through the cold, hood up and head down, back to my room, jumped into my bed and punched my pillow, shouting obscenities in the dark.

For some time I had been fighting my depression, psyching myself up in the morning with my Bruce Springsteen routine. Although in Boston I had cared nothing about music and had never bought a tape or record in my life, here these tapes which my family had sent me could,

50

in a crazy way, charge me, energize me in the early morning.

I would wake up, strip, turn on one of Bruce's tapes, plant my bare feet on the ice-cold shower tiles and dance naked, leap up and down, as the freezing water and Springsteen's songs covered my body and took over my mind.

Confronting my face in the mirror, I would talk to myself in the roles of coach/trainer and jock.

"You can do this, Jeff," the coach said.

"I'm the best!" I yelled back. "No one can stop me. No one!"

Maybe I was going nuts.

That night, to the music of "Born to Run" and "Thunder Road," I strutted and jumped and danced around the room, and imagined I was Bruce prancing up and down the stage at Giants Stadium in New Jersey, surrounded by women crazy for me, reaching up, touching me. Though I had declared her "dead" a few minutes ago, I sang to my girlfriend's picture; but Bruce's song is about splitting up with his girl.

I leaped from the stage and collapsed on my bed.

Voices.

Father Ricardo: "All they want is sandwiches."

My father: "None of these programs help the poor."

Back home my friends were with their girlfriends. They could see the Red Sox and Celtics play.

"What the hell am I doing?" I sobbed to myself. "You're a goddamn crybaby, Jeff. Get hold of yourself, man."

IX

Models of Resistance

One way to pull myself out of the awful mess I had made was to get a better experiential and intellectual sense of the revolution that had been shaking the church within Latin America and what other persons, long before I had discovered third world poverty, had been doing for the poor.

One was Father John Halligan, S.J. in Quito, Ecuador, who in 1962 began by serving free lunches and providing hot showers in the attic of the Jesuit church to the boys who worked in the streets. Today he directs the Working Boys' Center, two vast, elaborate complexes which teach carpentry, electronics, beauty, sewing and other trades, and provide primary and secondary education, health and spiritual care for working boys and other members of their families. Father Halligan also explained, when I visited him in July after my mother and grandmother had left, that the boys too had to assume responsibility for the center, contribute through their work, and adhere to rules or face expulsion.

In Quito I happened to pick up Ana Carrigan's *Salvador Witness: The Life and Calling of Jean Donovan* (1984), the biography of a young woman from Westport, Connecticut who went to El Salvador in 1979 to work as a lay missionary with the Maryknoll Sisters and who, on December 2, 1980, along with three other American missionary women, was raped and murdered by the Salvadoran military.

Our families were similar, yet different. Both were stable—in that my family, up to the divorce, gave the three of us a lot of love and have continued to support us since they separated. But Jean's parents were more pious than mine. Hers were Nixon Republicans and we were Democrats, although my father, who had Republican leanings, registered Democratic to vote for his father-in-law. I think Jean had more money than I did. For a few years after college and graduate school in economics, she had plunged into the career world—the good life of a management consultant at Arthur Andersen in Cleveland, a life which my friends had joined but which I, for a while, had put off.

But during her Mary Washington College junior year abroad at the University of the City of Cork, she met a sophisticated Irish priest, Father Michael Crowley, who had just returned from ten years living and working in the slums of Trujillo, on the northern desert coast of Peru. He would say: "It is a terrible tragedy to see the world powers reading as communism what is in fact nothing more than the cry of the poor for justice. If the free west really wants to contain communism worldwide, then it must attack injustice. If the west were to declare war on poverty and eliminate poverty, communism would be dead, because no one would believe it." With talk like that, Crowley caught the imaginations of young people and stirred up in Jean a long felt but seldom expressed desire to do missionary work.

When she gradually realized in the late 1970s that she had to make a break with the self-centered, party-loving, relatively wealthy but still insecure and immature person she had become, she flew back to Ireland for advice from Father Crowley. Soon afterward she began volunteer work for the diocese of Cleveland, and soon after that she committed herself for two years of missionary service in El Salvador.

53

She arrived during one of the bloodiest periods of Salvador's political and religious history.

In 1968, at a hemispheric conference of all the Latin American bishops at Medellín, Colombia, the church, realizing that its historic alignment with the generals, the wealthy land-owning classes, and the established and often corrupt economic and political structures had compromised its mission to spread the gospel, dramatically began to transform itself into the "church of the poor."

The theoretical basis for this transformation was called liberation theology, most fully laid out in the book *A Theology of Liberation* (1971) by the Peruvian priest-scholar, Gustavo Gutierrez; but the important thing for me—and, I think, for Jean Donovan as well—is that it is a theology based not just on scholarship but also on reflection on the day-to-day experiences of oppressed people. On the exploited farm workers and dead child in Ite, on my street kids, and on the murdered and mutilated peasants whom Jean and her co-workers helped the parish priest piece together, photograph and bury. On the death of Armando, twenty-three, a young man whom Jean loved and whom terrorists killed—shot in the mouth as he called for help beneath her window. She wrapped his bleeding body in her bed sheets. It is a theology that identifies the human person of Jesus Christ, who himself was a murder victim of an oppressive state, and therefore his church, with the lives of the poor.

The church immediately began to pay the price for its new message. In 1977, just two years before Jean arrived, Jesuit Father Rutilio Grande, the first priest after Medellín to abandon the life of a seminary professor and share the lives of peasants, was riddled with dum-dum bullets, the standard ammunition of the police and military guard, on his way to say evening mass. A popular bumper sticker appeared around the country: "BE A PATRIOT, KILL A PRIEST."

This began a wave of assassinations, which reached their most publicly terrible moment in the martyrdom of the archbishop of San Salvador, Oscar A. Romero, shot while saying mass on March 24, 1980. And it continues as this is written, when the overall death toll in El Salvador alone has risen to 70,000, including the widely publicized November 1989 massacre of six Jesuit scholars, their housekeeper, and her daughter.

I knew that in no way could my own life and work in Peru approach the heroism which this other young person from Connecticut gradually achieved, but I focused on what we had in common—the desire to do something more with our lives than the American good life of the 1970s and 1980s would let us; the battle with loneliness relieved in confronting the endless needs of those we tried to serve. Jean's friends had tried to dissuade her from returning to El Salvador after a visit home, but she wrote to a friend two weeks before she was shot in the back of the head: "Several times I have decided to leave El Salvador. I almost could except for the children, the poor, bruised victims of this insanity. Who would care for them? Whose heart could be so staunch as to favor the reasonable thing in a sea of their tears and loneliness? Not mine, dear friend, not mine."

Closer to home, I learned that Father Fred, too—though on a less brutal level—had been a victim of the same system, when he had dared to stand up against the government of General Juan Velasco Alvarado, who had seized power as head of a junta in 1968. In Father Fred's judgment, the Velasco government had, in some ways, been a responsible one. Velasco changed Peruvian history with a land reform that put an end to the domination of the large landowners, but he had curtailed freedom of the press and his military build-up seemed headed toward another conflict with Chile. When he fell ill in 1975, he was removed from office in another coup and died in 1976.

In 1970 Father Fred had written a letter—signed by all the Cristo Rey teachers and circulated and reported throughout the country—which criticized the Velasco regime when it raised the salaries of army officers but not of teachers. As a result, the teachers went on strike and won concessions, but the Velasco government retaliated by trying to throw Father Fred out of the country. Only the personal intervention of Bishop Luis Bambaren, S.J. of Chimbote, who admired Father Fred's work, convinced Velasco that it would be politically foolish to expel the city's most respected citizen.

I cannot testify to a startling conversion experience, but gradually in mid-1986, day by day I began to change —in a process that corresponded in many ways to the changes transforming the church itself. On the intellectual level, reading books like Gutierrez's and Penny Lernoux's *Cry of the People* (1982), which chronicles the emergence of a new democracy, the new theology and a new church throughout Latin America, provided a rational foundation for what I was undergoing sensibly, emotionally—particularly when I went to mass.

On a Saturday night, in a pueblo joven called (true to the Latin American penchant for paradoxical names) "Belo Horizonte," in a chapel the poor had built themselves, a small room, lit by one bulb and covered with a thatch roof, thirty people, mostly women and children, sat on benches around a wooden table altar. A young Jesuit, Father Santiago Vallebuona, began the liturgy by asking them what they would like to pray about.

As he wrote their petitions with a magic marker on a paper stuck to a styrofoam bulletin board, they said they wanted to pray for their sick friends, for some priests who had been thrown out of Chile, for me and my companion, and for the success of their barbecue to raise funds for more church benches. In dialogue with us, Santiago showed how the gospel of the multiplication of the loaves and fishes demonstrated not so much Christ's miraculous power as the power of the people, through work and selflessness, to transform their own lives—to get a better school, trees, a park.

I began to see the power of the gospel message for the poor: Jesus' life was revolutionary; his disciples were poor—farmers and fishermen awakened to new possibilities within themselves. Jesus died because he dared to tell the poor they had a right to a better life. He had dared to stand up in the synagogue and say: "The spirit of the Lord has been given to me, for he has anointed me. He has sent me to preach the good news to the poor, to proclaim liberty to captives, and to the blind new sight, to set the downtrodden free, to proclaim the Lord's year of favor" (Lk 4:18–19).

Whenever I thought of giving up, and when Springsteen began to sound stale, that's what I read.

He's grounded in faith

X

One Strange Night

In its first months, after opening in mid-August, 1986, the new Center for the Working Child did little good.

Frankly, we—my team of high school students and student teachers—in spite of the prolonged dialogues in which we tried to define our goals, had refurbished the building and opened our doors without clear decisions on what we were trying to do.

Give these children an escape from the streets? Feed them? Reform their personalities and behavior? Make them better Catholics?

So we improvised. We tried lectures, table soccer, games, catechism classes, free lunch and dinner—with an unenforceable no-class-no-food requirement. But they remained true to their acquired natures. Thieves by profession, besides ripping off hubcaps and auto parts in the streets, they also stole from us; when we fought, which was often, they turned on water spigots and flooded the floor, urinated and wrote obscenities on the wall which I had to clean off. They clogged our prized flush toilet which I was continually teaching them to use.

When female student teachers came to work in the food line—but too often just to gawk at me—the boys called them whores and once grabbed their breasts. When one of my Cristo Rey boys, a weak, spoiled do-gooder who usually tried to get on a teacher's good side by telling on his peers, tried to help me maintain order, a working boy punched him in the testicles and sent him bawling and limping home.

When I threw them out they pelted the walls with rocks and disrupted traffic in the street by playing a Peruvian version of "chicken": they stood in the center of the street and faced down oncoming buses and cars, jumped on their hoods and roofs, and banged their sides and windshields.

But I liked them and, in spite of their insults, they seemed to like me. Throughout this, I thought there were passing moments when we were getting somewhere. One night Juan Carlos, who had been one of our most destructive guests, pleaded with me to protect him from his older brother, a soldier, who beat him at home and pursued him to the Center.

I confronted the young man in uniform. "I'm on leave," he said. "His mother wants him back. So I hit him. His father isn't around."

I made him promise he wouldn't hit him again. I was gaining their trust. Sometimes they would simply call me on the phone and ask me how I was doing.

They had been treated on a sub-human level for so long, I thought, they had been conditioned to respond violently to any situation that confused them. When I took little Oscar, called "chicken" because of the way his eyes sunk deep into his hollow-cheeked face, to the hospital with a cut foot, the doctor remarked: "He's like an animal, isn't he?"

I once watched when a fat lady who wasn't satisfied with the shoe shine she was getting from Gringo, Oscar's pale-faced pal, blustered, "You boys are dirty and ugly. Ugly, ugly. I can't stand to look at you."

When she had paid him, Gringo spit at her feet and grunted, "Mierda!" (Shit!) to her. I thought it was the most dignified thing he could do.

They were wonderful! They were curing my depression, teaching me to be thankful for what I had and to laugh at things that were out of my control.

The more involved I became with the poor, the more I tried to break down the divisions—both economic and social—between the rich and poor students at Cristo Rey. Consistent with school policy, I required them to work at the Center for social responsibility credits; I lectured daily on injustices I saw in Peruvian society and even told them they should stop segregating themselves according to social class in the lunch room.

The biggest obstacle was the parents. Most of them shuddered at the thought that their sons might actually spend productive years of their lives trying to modify the economic system the parents had put in place. When they learned of my tirades, some supported me and even gave money to the Center, while others thought I was crazy. When I gave one boy who had just lazed around the Center a low grade for social responsibility and wrote on his evaluation that he wasn't leading an active Christian life, his mother was indignant: "How can you say my son isn't a good Christian? Every morning I make him pray in front of the statue of the Virgin Mary!"

In one strange, unpredictable evening, I moved between sundown and dawn through two contrasting social worlds.

I had been planning to spend the evening at the home of some wealthy benefactors, the D'Angelos (not their real name), Italian immigrants, who had a son, Pedro, in my class. But the mother, Maria, called to cancel—she had a friend visiting from out of town—and asked me to sub for her as the godparent at the baptism of the school gardener's son.

For a lot of reasons, this I was not anxious to do. Baptisms are big events, and I wasn't up to an all-night party.

Being a godparent in Peru means being a real patron, getting the boy established in life; and I was in no position to
do that. Besides, the gardener, Javier, was no saint. He was
a drunk, was said to hit his wife, and often turned violent
with other school employees.

But Maria said please, and I said yes.

Javier's party was a big one; some of his nephews had
been baptized as well. Indeed, the grand style of their
party belied their poverty. The family and guests all
sported suit coats, ties, and highly polished shoes—with
me the worst dressed, in my standard plaid shirt and blue
jeans. Javier and his wife had probably spent two months
of their joint income to entertain us in a four-room shack
with a dirt-floor dining room; we had wine, dark beer,
picante (a hot and spicy mix of cow's intestines and potatoes), steak, potatoes, salad, and more beer and wine. Behind the kitchen, two lambs, a dog and some children
played and tried to jump the fence and join the fun.

Suddenly Maria D'Angelo and her friend from out of
town waltzed in. It would have been rude, the friend said,
not to go to the party. The music went up, the dancing
pulled everyone in. But, worn out, we made for the door
—only to be overtaken by Javier, with four beer bottles
tucked under his arm, who made the three of us join him
for one more brew.

No, of course I could not go home now, Maria cooed; I
had to come to their party too. The beer and wine had
already done their damage, and I, in a slightly dizzy state,
was now open for something a little more intimate and
relaxed.

But in the D'Angelo residence I entered a dazzlingly
different world. Two maids bustled about with trays of
drinks and hors d'oeuvres. In the back of the house,
through the large glass sliding doors, the turquoise surface
of the swimming pool, with the handball court and gardens
in the background, shimmered in the soft outdoor lights.
Pedro, my pupil, who cowered in the corner absorbed

with his computer, acknowledged my greeting with his usual shy, embarrassed smile.

By the bar facing the pool, the host, Carlo D'Angelo, stood wielding a bourbon and water, absorbed in talk with a heavy-set friend he introduced to me as Mr. Vasquez.

Within a few moments I was working on a bourbon and water too, and the burly Vasquez, by this hour a little wobbly on his feet, had grabbed me by the arm and led me away to the other side of the pool. He wanted "to talk."

"Look," he said. "You're a professional teacher. Right?"

I protested that I was really very amateur, but he didn't listen and said it again.

"Look," he said, as he leaned forward, grabbed my shoulder, and glared at me for what seemed several minutes, his bourbon breath close enough to make me cough. Maybe he's going to confess something, I thought.

"Look," he said for the third time. "Do you think Carlo's boy, Pedro, is all right? I mean, do you think he's a little . . . strange?" He extended his hand and turned it, in an ambiguous gesture, from side to side.

"I think he's a good boy," I said. Glancing over Vasquez's broad shoulder, back through the glass doors, I could see the boy's round shoulders huddled over the silver, glimmering video screen.

"Yea, a good boy. But he's a little . . . you know, he could turn out queer some day. And that's a horrible thing."

The boy was a little effeminate, but I saw nothing abnormal in him. I couldn't believe I was in this conversation.

"Look, I've got a kid Pedro's age. He's real strong. He swears, yells, fights, insults people, goes out with girls, knows Lima well. He's a real man. Carlo's my best friend and I want his kid to turn out all right. You get what I mean?"

I got what he meant. But my main goal was to get out

of this awful session. I promised that I, Pedro's teacher, would help the boy become a "man."

With a drunken, beaming smile and a knowing wink, Vasquez put his arm around me gratefully. "I love Carlo. I'd hate to have to tell him his son was queer."

I don't know what he expected me to do—maybe escort the lad to a whorehouse, which in some Peruvian families is an acceptable form of sexual initiation. To the chagrin of young Americans like myself who spend time in Peru, this image of the chauvinistic, dominating, Peruvian male is a cultural given, perpetuated by both Peruvian men and women.

A few minutes later, as we rejoined the party, Mr. D'Angelo himself, his face flushed with emotion and late night spirits, seized me, led me to the bar, sloshed more bourbon into my glass, and, rambling on about a lot of things, told me how he loved and admired his long-time friend Vasquez.

"Listen," he said, grabbing my arm as Vasquez had, suddenly changing his tone, his voice harder. "You went to that baptism. I never go to those baptisms. You want to know why?"

He was going to tell me whether I wanted to hear it or not.

"Because those people in the pueblos jovenes are liars, thieves, pigs, no good. You understand? They're worth shit." With his stiff forefinger he repeatedly poked my chest.

"They're bastards," he growled, raising his voice a few decibels. "When I came from Italy, I wanted to help those people. I gave them food. I gave them jobs. But they screwed me." He was very angry and very drunk. "They kill their friends and rape women. Maria always wants me to help them, so I pay for things. But I can't stand the liars. You think you can help those people. But you can't. Do you get that? It isn't worth it. Forget about them."

So that was it. He wanted me to stop my work. I was in

63

his home, drinking his bourbon; he was mad, and I saw no sense in arguing with him.

He paused, staggered, waited for a response. "Salud," I said, raising my half-empty glass, and we had another drink together. At table we dined on soup, salad, lamb, potatoes, wine, cake, and ice cream. At 1:30 A.M. some of Mr. D'Angelo's friends who had stayed sober delivered me back to Cristo Rey.

It was becoming increasingly clear that if I was to accomplish anything in Peru, it would have to be through working more with people like Javier and less with the D'Angelos and their son.

XI

From One Home to Another

One of the worst things about travel is the incommunicability, and ultimately the alienating effect, of the experience. We can tell our friends that we have been to the other side of the moon and they can reply yes, yes, isn't that interesting, that must have been a "really incredible trip." But if they themselves have not been to the moon or to Peru or even Bermuda or New York—have not been shaken by what to us was in a way akin to death and rebirth—or if they are not exceptionally sensitive persons who can learn from what someone else has seen and felt, our travels end up isolating us from old companions, even family. They don't understand, we end up saying to ourselves. They just don't understand.

As Christmas 1986 drew near, I knew that my family wanted me to come home. Several relatives were ill, and it was likely that this was the last time I could see them. And I wanted to see Jill—to test what in our relationship had been able to survive the separation, her failure to visit when I needed her, her extended silences, my obsessive absorption in my work and the series of emotional shocks that had radically shaken up how I looked at an American value system which many of my friends took as more precious and authoritative than the Old and New Testament.

My grandparents and Mike Kuntz, who gave me a big hug, met me in Miami, where I indulged in my first hot shower in five months; and then Jill met me when I flew into Boston.

For a while our reunion was awkward. But she had come to the airport to pick me up. I was wrong to be mad at her for so long. She now had my old job as president of the Undergraduate Government and had a lot to worry about besides me in Peru. After all, I was the one who had gone away. As we drew near to Boston College turf in Chestnut Hill we loosened up; we were on familiar territory. And there we settled into a favorite seafood restaurant, the kind of place that used to help determine the tone of our social lives; it gave our set that warm, comfy feeling, the confidence that we were with people who knew and loved us and that we were going to make our mark in the world when we "got out."

But as we ordered—appetizers, clams, oysters, catch of the day—a shot of the slum behind Cristo Rey, the one I had seen on my first day there, flashed across my eyes.

Jill was talking to me, but I was talking to myself: "Man, this wealth is sick. This wealth is sick." The noise level seemed to rise—a chatter chatter of English, which now struck me as a foreign language, with women in pearls, men in expensive suits, waiters and waitresses slinking and sliding from table to table.

After dinner we wandered for fifteen minutes—all I could endure—at the Chestnut Hill Mall, a place where some of the wealthiest people in the world shop. As children under five in Latin America died every twenty seconds, I strolled through a mall decorated with huge Santa Clauses and three hundred dollar sweaters and a place called Odessa that sold hundred dollar tea kettles and a glass ball with flashing lights inside for one thousand dollars.

I grabbed Jill and we ran from the site. The year before I had celebrated Christmas with a humble mass in a slum, with hot chocolate, and fruit cake.

My "home" now was, in a sense, two "homes," since my now divorced parents were establishing new, independent lives for themselves and my role was to graciously meet their new "companions." At family gatherings I was the novelty. I was skinnier and wore sideburns, until I shaved them off to keep my sister happy. With family friends I had not seen in years and even with college friends, I felt as if I were a museum piece, and I must have appeared dumb and flustered when asked to describe Tacna and its children by people who had no comprehension of where Peru was—"Oh yeah, that's over there by Spain, isn't it?"—or what I was trying to do.

One person asked me to pick him up some cocaine on my next trip. Another warned me about the "commies" who were taking over Central America and Miami.

Another was utterly nonplussed that the same guy who was student president at B.C. could be wasting his time "down there" for an allowance of eighty-five dollars a month. "What's the deal?"

Another took me aside at a party. "Jeff, I admire what you're doing, but I just couldn't do it. I just love money too much. I love money a lot. It's that simple. You know what I mean?"

Another assured me that once I got this out of my system I'd be doing contracts and real estate law like the rest of them and making big bucks too. "We all look forward to that day."

Another friend told me he was saddened by his cat's illness, so to make it feel better he had made it a Christmas dinner of flounder and white wine.

And a relative bought the family dog steaks for its New Year's Day meal. In Peru, in the pueblos jovenes, thousands—millions—of scrawny dogs range through the dirt scrounging for scraps to live on. For a while the families use them as protectors. Sometimes they use them for a meal.

So I returned to Tacna and a second month of social service in January all the more determined to make our project work, as an answer, an alternative, to what I had seen and heard in Boston and Meriden.

Somehow during this second social service project I had better control of the students. When I returned to the Center, which I had left in the hands of student teachers, I found that its supervisors had let things deteriorate in my absence. It still wasn't strong enough to function without me. But by April and May we had a real sense of progress. We cut the free food to bread and milk daily and lunch on Saturday for a small fee. The new art classes, suggested by a kid called Kickers, were teaching dozens of boys to turn seashells into animals, boats, insects and ashtrays they could sell. We sponsored a trip to a cultural conference in Lima for a boy who had not flown in a plane or left home since his mother brought him to Tacna as a baby.

But our project moved into a new phase with the arrival of Bertha Pantigoso, the professional social worker sent by the city government, who had worked in agrarian reform in Puno under the Velasco administration, who had learned the Aymara language then, and who was now equipped to research the family backgrounds of the fifty boys who were our steady clientele. She was a short, stout, middle-aged woman who liked to take charge and run things according to her own time schedule, and who had great empathy for the mothers struggling to keep their families together. The women, in turn, adored her.

We learned that many families were fatherless, that single mothers had six to eight children to care for, that the mothers fed them on potato and vegetable stew, tea and bread, that they lived by selling vegetables and contraband and by washing clothes, and that there was a rumor around that "this gringo had started this Center and was going to take all the children to the United States."

Systematically, Bertha made the rounds, intervening in family fights, above all trying to get the boys to go to school. She met one boy's mother coming out of a house of prostitution—that's where she worked—and together we had to "denounce" the mother and file a suit against her to force her to assume responsibility for her son.

But soon we had discovered a new dimension of the problem and, consequently, a new clientele: mothers. Mothers had not made school a priority for their children because their main worry was simply getting enough to eat.

Maria Rivera, for example, had five children. Her husband had died the year before we met her while she was pregnant with the fifth. The oldest girl worked as a maid. Only Jose Luis, eleven, a very bright lad who shined shoes and hung out at the Center, attended school. Her husband's property was still not in Maria's name, and she couldn't afford the clothing, books and pens the others would need if they wanted an education.

Agripina Vargas and her three children, one of whom was retarded, lived together in a straw hut where they all shared the same bed. The children's father was a married man who contributed nothing to their support.

Estefania Mamani was tougher; when her husband walked out on her and their four children she got a court order requiring support payments every month.

Meanwhile hundreds of mothers like these made the rounds of the several agencies and groups set up to help them, learning to cook together in one program and sew together in another. We added ourselves to this network. In mid-1987 we opened up weaving and knitting classes, and once a week Bertha organized the women to make "sopapillas," fried dough to feed the children. Almost without intending it, we were developing another community. To the boys, Bertha was becoming the stern and caring mother some of them never knew; to the mothers, she was an older sister—someone to come to when their husbands beat them or their children disobeyed.

It was in March of that year that I decided that if I was to be consistent, follow my principles one more step and really identify with the Peruvian people, I should move into a pueblo joven myself. Furthermore, Bonnie and Leigh had not signed up for a second year as volunteers, and I was now more alone than ever at Cristo Rey.

I joined the family of Genoveva Williams de Herrera, a widowed mother of eight daughters, seven of whom lived in Lima, and one son, Victor, a high school student. The other daughter, Nelly, was married to Juan Carlos Diaz, who worked in a bank, and lived at home. The five of us shared a simple, three-bedroom cement block house with a tin roof, cold-running-water bathroom, living room and outdoor kitchen where we cooked over a kerosene stove.

Genoveva's father was an English miner who had married her mother in Bolivia, sired Genoveva and her sister, and then announced that he was going back to England for a visit to get money for the family—and was never seen again. At fourteen Genoveva married a Peruvian, Victor Herrera, and they moved to Lima, and then to Tacna, where in the 1960s they joined an "invasion," a sudden, mass expropriation of unpopulated land, of the area next to the new Colegio Cristo Rey. According to custom, they joined with their neighbors to develop the area over the years, adding water, light and paving, building their straw huts by stages into relatively comfortable homes.

When Victor, a bus driver, was killed in a crash during a night run to Lima, Genoveva raised the children herself. She sold food, raised chickens, and took in boarders—like me. So I was part of a family. I laughed with Juan Carlos, a Cristo Rey alumnus, when he told his high school stories. I joined in the local political gossip, and listened to young Victor plan ways to dodge his Peruvian military obligation —an "obligation" which the well-to-do managed to avoid through either bribery or a college exemption.

We lived on a diet of mostly oatmeal, bread, fruit and tea—occasionally supplemented by chicken, rice, fish or meat stew. In the evenings we sat around the black-and-white TV and watched the news—including President Alan Garcia's attempt to nationalize the banks, a move which led many to conclude that this once charismatic young messiah had gone "loco," and which prompted the famous novelist, Mario Vargas Llosa, author of *Conversations in the Cathedral* (1969), *The War at the End of the World* (1984) and *Aunt Julia and the Scriptwriter*, based on his own youthful, short-lived first marriage to his aunt, to announce that he was running for president.

It was an important moment in Peruvian political history. I remembered the bureaucrat in Ite who longed for a "strong man" to set things right, and I wondered if the populace was ready to fall in behind this former communist, once an admirer of the Cuban revolution, whose heroes now were Charles de Gaulle and Margaret Thatcher. On the TV screen and in a series of slick commercials designed by American ad men, he was a handsome man, a romantic figure. But to his critics he was more European than Peruvian, a front man for the old Lima elite who were using him to regain privileges lost in a series of liberal reforms.

"It doesn't matter who's in office," Genoveva said. "They're all corrupt. We keep on going without them."

When the daughters visited from Lima, where they had become prosperous enough to dress sharply and wear lipstick and jewelry, they liked to cluster around me and ask me personal questions. When one of the single ones tried to get me aside for herself, their mother hovered nearby, protecting me as if I were her son.

"Do you like Peruvian women?" the daughter asked.

71

"Sure."

"Good. Then wouldn't you want to take one to America with you?"

I smiled and tried to change the subject.

"Do you like sleeping in your room all alone? Wouldn't you like some company? You in your room all alone just makes me feel sad."

Genoveva ran interference for me, and I was glad. When I attended Saturday evening mass I could never understand why Tacna's teenagers all crowded around me after mass and found me so attractive. It was probably because my skin was white and I was from a different country.

My real social life was, now that I think of it, a throwback to Boston College: long Friday night drinking bouts with the Cristo Rey male faculty at Torcazas, a simple local bar with nothing but a few tables and chairs and lots of beer, particularly a great Peruvian beer called "Cusquena." This we consumed by the quart as we told classroom war stories, bragged about how great we were, and bitched about the colleagues and Jesuits we didn't like—those who were lazy or soft, who didn't give much homework, or who disappeared during the workday when they should have been with the kids.

As the night wore on we yelled louder and louder and waved our arms in the hot, smoke-filled air; then sometimes after three quarts I would simply tilt forward and fall asleep while the others raved on around me.

But I could never fall asleep for long on my best friend, a math teacher, Edgar Durand. One July night in 1987 he and I celebrated our National Teachers Day raise and bonus by blowing most of it, first at Torcazas, where "El Gordo" served us beer after beer till he closed, then at the "Sky Room," the seventh floor pub of a posh tourist hotel, where we switched to pisco sours.

I remember that I got Edgar to his house where I carried him out of the cab and handed him over to his mother, and that I didn't have enough money to pay the cabbie when I arrived home, and said I would make it up to him sometime.

I stumbled into our house where Genoveva had left a bowl of hot oatmeal and bread for me on the living room table. I'm not sure what happened next. The room began to spin around, and my head pitched forward, my face plopped down into the bowl of porridge sitting in front of me, and I fell asleep with my face in the gruel.

If Genoveva had not come out later, lifted my head, wiped me off, and put me to bed, I might have suffocated.

XII

We Decide to Grow

"Promise me you're coming home, Jeff," she said. "I can't keep waiting like this. It just isn't fair."

A year had passed since I stood cursing at her picture and wailing Bruce Springsteen, and now, in July–August 1987, finally, with my mother and grandmother, Jill had come to Peru. We had all traveled together for a week— we had taken the perilous train ride to Machu Picchu— and Jill had stayed a few more days so we could talk. Now, as we headed for the airport and another good-bye, she wanted some firm understanding of how long I was going to drag this project out.

"I promise," I said. "Don't worry. I'll be home before you know it."

Technically my two year stint was up in December. But I had been plagued by two big questions: What would happen when we had to return the property to Garcia in July 1988, and what would happen to the Center when I went home?

My answers were that we needed new land to build an expanded, permanent Center and a commitment from Cristo Rey to maintain it as part of its apostolate. So I wrote my parents telling them that I had to extend my stay to March 1988 so that I could build a new Center and train my successors, the volunteers who would arrive in October 1987. Then I would go to law school.

But as I drove home from the airport I wondered how I could possibly live up to what I had said.

When I got back to my room I sat at my typewriter and banged out a letter to the mayor of Tacna, Tito Chocano, from Father Fred Green, S.J., superior of the Jesuit community, asking for a new 800 to 1,000 square meter piece of land for the Center for the Working Child.

In fact I had tried to induce Fred to sign a similar letter months before, but he had put me off on the grounds that he had to consult the Jesuit community. "Yeah, but let's see if we can get the land first," I said. "If we do get it, then we can meet with the community and talk about it."

This time he went along—although I knew that if we got the land, we wouldn't consult. We'd build.

After almost two months of my usual annoying politicking and daily pestering of the city hall functionaries in their offices, I learned that the mayor had orally agreed to grant us a triangular strip of land in the northwestern corner of the town, near the city's cemeteries, coliseum, stadium, and new bus terminal—an ideal site where working street kids, many of whom were paid to water flowers at gravestones, would congregate. It was a 1,200 square meter plot in the tip of a larger 14,000 square meter barren area which the city planned to develop as a commercial center. This was almost too good to be true.

In September Cristo Rey celebrated its twenty-fifth anniversary, and Father Fred retired as director of the school and kept the position as superior of the Jesuit community. The new director, Father John P. Foley, S.J., who had first come to Peru as a scholastic (an unordained Jesuit still in studies) in 1961, took charge. We knew his arrival would amount to a big boost for the Center when he visited the scene in October and exclaimed enthusiastically, "I'm behind this. This is what we Jesuits are all about. Let's go for it."

If Father Fred and Father John were different personalities, they complemented each other. While Fred was slender and reserved, John was a big, gray-haired, fun-loving man in his early fifties who would fight a losing battle

Top: Women digging footings for one of the buildings at the Cristo Rey Center. The women were paid during the week, but volunteered their time on Sundays. **Bottom:** Jeff Thielman outside the Center's main building, completed in February, 1989.

with his waistline with daily jogging and basketball, and then unwind with a few beers.

My father came down for the four-day anniversary festival, and I assured him that I would be home by April at the latest. Father John mentioned later on what I had not been observant enough to record: how fully my father devoted himself to me and all that we were doing while he was here.

As we planned for the new Center, we had everything but the legal title to the property, a document the mayor had said he would give us but which for some reason he couldn't get around to drawing up.

Finally I had to call his hand. A woman named Marianne Persianoff, a filmmaker, had come to do a documentary on Father Fred, had fallen in love with the children at the Center, and had offered to do a fund-raising video on our project. I sent word to the mayor that, for the benefit of American viewers, we needed a scene in the film that demonstrated that we had the land, that we had scripted a segment where he presents us with a document—a mayoral resolution we could draw up reserving the plot for the Center—and that this was his chance to be seen on American TV.

So in early November, with Marianne's camera whirring, Mayor Chocano signed the resolution and handed it to Fred Green and me. The ceremony never appeared in the film, but it was the trick we needed to get the land and give the Center a permanent home.

One of my friends on the city council, Leopoldo Meyer, a businessman who also taught English at Cristo Rey, explained to me that the document wasn't a property title but was good enough to start with.

I don't think I knew what a property title was. Whatever we had was good enough for me.

XIII

Tricked

Father Fred had twenty-five years of construction experience in Peru. He leaned back in his chair during one of our regular late evening chats, looked me in the eye, and said in his calm, grandfatherly way, "You don't know what you're getting into, Jeff. You're going to learn a lot . . . more than you can ever imagine. Live and learn. That's the idea."

Some of my problems from then on were due to things I couldn't control, like Peru's economic crisis. Inflation in 1988 hovered around 1800 percent. As the Shining Path stepped up their attacks on cities and country towns, disrupting transportation and power supplies, shortages of basic goods, including food, increased. In some areas children were threatened with starvation. There was not enough cement or iron to allow us to start building until January.

Nor did I have enough money. Because of her illness, Marianne's fund-raising video wouldn't be ready till April. So we had to depend on my begging letters, which ultimately brought in a five thousand dollar gift from an anonymous American businessman, and on a local entrepreneur who was to become our number one angel, Jorge Llontop, a short, pudgy dynamo who could talk on two phones at once, and who promised to lend me whatever I wanted without interest. Jorge was to become my mentor and sidekick during this whole adventure.

His youngest daughter had died of leukemia in 1985, and he wanted to invest in something that would employ the poor. Earlier he had given me weaving looms and a sewing machine so the mothers could learn to manufacture sweaters; now he was teaching me how to determine exactly how much money I needed and to ask for it.

My other problems stemmed from my own bad judgment, ignorance and inexperience. It was bad judgment to pick Mario Bacigalupo, the Lima architect who had designed the Colegio's athletic facility, to design the Center and to accept his decision to build the outside walls with adobe, which he said was cheaper, rather than cement blocks, which had been generally used since the 1960s. Following his formula, to make adobe bricks we had to mix mud, straw and asphalt, place the mixture in a mold, and let it dry for three weeks. One of my jobs was to drive around town looking for cement for our outside walls and three times a week to fill tin drums with asphalt and kerosene.

As I biked from one cement distributor to another, begging, one called out, "Go home, son. You're going to go crazy here."

When we discovered that twenty percent of the adobe bricks crumbled when we tried to move them, and that in the long run the adobe wall was a thousand dollars more expensive than one made with cement bricks, I almost did go crazy.

Nevertheless, while we built a new one, the original Center was still growing. It was always full of boys, due in large part to the arrival of the popular new volunteers, Lou Harrington and Bill Peters, who started swimming lessons and trips to local factories for the kids. We stabilized the daily hot lunch program, started reading and writing classes for illiterate mothers, and, with help from the Immaculate Heart of Mary nuns, prepared thirty-three children from the Center for baptism.

Furthermore, Lou and Bill were good for me. I moved

my residence back to the school to be with them, and they challenged me night after night, sometimes bitterly, to spell out more clearly my vision for the future. "We've got all kinds of people going through there every day," shouted Bill one night, "and just about everybody comes just for the food and television. What are we going to do?"

The fact was that I never had definitively spelled out a blueprint for the future. I was improvising by responding to needs as I perceived them. That's all I knew how to do.

Now, as time grew short and my parents continued to call and ask when I was coming home, I was beginning to wonder if I ever really could go home. Part of it was that I was just beginning to comprehend what creating a Center involved. Bill had made his point. And I was petrified that after I left someone would ask, "What happened to that thing the Gringo tried to start for the shoeshine boys?" The Center was more important to me than all I had left behind in the United States, and that was not easy to explain to the folks back home.

But my biggest mistake slowly began to reveal itself when the architect and I began to realize that the land we had asked for was not enough for the soccer court, not enough for fifty kids to run around in, not enough to satisfy the expanding dreams we had for our enterprise. The first two times that we asked for ten meters here or there, my city hall contact, Leopoldo, came back with an O.K. But the third time the mayor stonewalled. "The registrar's office needs that plot," he said. "Besides, there'll be a new park for your kids to run around in."

But when I told the registrar we would be neighbors she said no, she was going over by the university. When I collared Leopoldo at coffee about the contradiction, he looked half-hostile, half-scared. "Look, don't get involved in this issue. You hear? Back off!"

I soon learned why.

During the third week of February, the contractor

told me some military men had visited the site and wanted to know what we were doing on their property.

On Thursday, February 25, I received an order from the city to stop work. The military had filed a complaint. When I tracked down Leopoldo he bluntly reminded me that the "resolution" we had so triumphantly videotaped did not give us title to the property. It was the military's land and they had yet to give it to the city. The horrible weight of this sank in. We had outsmarted the mayor, tricked him into "giving us" the land. But we had been tricked. We were building on land we didn't own.

Thousands of dollars had been raised and spent for nothing. Wait till they hear about this back home, I thought.

XIV

The Three Sisters

I loomed over the mayor's desk. I had liked him. He was a fat, good-humored farmer in leather jacket and tinted glasses who had a big enough heart to give us a social worker, and his wife Teresa had given us donations for the soup kitchen. But he was patronizing me—for some reason, lying to me. The city engineers had read the map wrong, he said. They had told him it was city land. "Don't worry, 'hermanito' (little brother)," he said. "Just keep working. Don't worry about the military. They always give us a hard time. We're getting the land. We'll trade some land with them. I'll tell you what I'm going to do."

He leaned back in his chair, swaggering his little, plump form, signaling to the naive gringo that he was an important person. "I shall write personally to the minister of defense, Enrique Lopez Albujar, and ask for his assistance in this matter. Will that satisfy you?"

A few days later, when I asked for a copy of the letter, he put me off. "Don't worry, hermanito. It's being taken care of."

Father John Foley ordered us to stop building until the issue was resolved.

Backed by an ad-hoc group we called the pro-construction committee, which included Jorge Llontop, several businessmen, and the mayor's wife, we began to devise a strategy to make our case to the minister of defense.

To our good fortune, living in Tacna in retirement, in a modest but attractive little home, surrounded by family heirlooms and artifacts, were the daughters of a famous Peruvian poet and national figure, the three sisters of Enrique Lopez Albujar. One was a widow, the other two single, their ages ranging from their late sixties to mid-seventies. They had all been school teachers. In fact, one of our committee, Lily Morales, a former member of the city council, had been the pupil of one of the three.

So, within a few days, Jorge, Lily and I found ourselves one afternoon in the three sisters' living room, balancing teacups on our knees, eating little cakes and listening in nervous awe as they chatted on in the very precise Spanish of the upper class, each in her turn, about their teaching days, politics, cooking, how Tacna had changed, and, of course, their brother the minister of defense.

"So you are the young man who is building this Center," Chavela Lopez Albujar said, as she pulled herself erect and looked at me very directly.

"Yes," I said, as I smiled and blushed a little.

"Que lindo! (How beautiful!)," she exclaimed. "You are a nice looking boy, I must say."

I smiled again and she pinched my cheek. It was like being with my aunts.

Stammering around for something else to talk about, I asked who had made some of the handicraft—paintings, lace tablecloths—which decorated their home.

"Well, I did," Beatrice Lopez Albujar announced with pride.

"They're very lovely," I said.

"Do you really think so?" Thus began a fifteen minute tour of the living room, dining room and hallway, with their hanging wall pieces, original paintings, lace and pottery.

"Que lindo," Chavela said again with a smile.

Throughout the small talk, the sisters said that they understood the urgency of our situation. Chavela sat down and wrote a letter to their brother asking him to help us get the property. "We're all teachers," Chavela said. "If it's for the children, we'll do all we can to help."

"Please come again," they said together as we departed, confident for the first time that events had turned slightly in our direction.

But I, for one, was still determined to get my hands on whatever documents the mayor had actually sent to the capital at Lima. As Jorge said to me privately, "I wouldn't be surprised if the mayor was trying to get that land for himself."

With my politician grandfather's blood heating up in my veins, I started making my rounds at city hall. The mayor's secretary, Doris, claimed that the mayor didn't have the paper work; it was over at the office of the city engineer, Wilmer Espinoza.

I knew Espinoza. He was a short, dark-haired, pudgy-faced little character with wire-rimmed glasses, who never looked you in the eye. Like the mayor, he had told me not to worry, and, like the mayor, he had denied having the papers. Gazing out the window as he spoke, he had told me, "Don't worry, hermanito. Everything will be all right."

Doris called Espinoza's secretary to smooth the way for me. I even zoomed past Espinoza as I raced up the stairs on the way to his office and hoped he didn't decide to turn around and come back to see what I was up to.

Espinoza's secretary said she couldn't find the plans.

"What do you mean you can't find the land plans?" I pleaded with her. "They have to be here. The mayor, Wilmer, the minister, everybody wants me to have a copy of this stuff. If we can't find it in the file cabinets, we should look through his desk. If I don't have this information there will be big problems."

"Oh, I can't do that," she squirmed nervously. "Wilmer won't like this."

"Por favor," I purred softly as I cocked my head to the side and frowned a little sadly, as Peruvians do when they want something an authority is trying to deny them. I flashed my most charming smile.

"Let's see," she replied, as we frantically began plundering his desk, opening drawer after drawer, rifling through his folders. What I was doing wasn't legally correct, I suppose. There was an odd morality to the whole scene. But I told myself I was a Peruvian Robin Hood, robbing a gutless bureaucrat to help the poor whom he and his fellow conspirators had defrauded.

I found it! When I read it my head spun. In it the mayor was asking the military to grant the whole tract, fourteen thousand square meters, to the city for the Center for the Working Child. But the original resolution had granted us only twelve hundred square meters. In short, he was trying to grab most of the land for himself under the pretext of giving it to a noble social project. It also meant that we now had a shot at ten times as much land as we had asked for in the first place.

"Please don't tell anyone about this," the young secretary implored.

I told her what the mayor and Wilmer had told me—not to worry—as I bounded downstairs to make copies.

Meanwhile Jorge, who had gone to Lima, had failed to get through to the minister of defense to plead our case. But we learned that the minister himself was due to visit Tacna on Saturday, March 26, for his annual review of the defense forces. So it was time for another of our several follow-up visits to the sisters, but this time—since the sisters attended the Jesuit church and held the fathers in high esteem—with Father John Foley, S.J. as part of the delegation.

John had had a tough week. He had expelled two students from the school because they had failed to show up too many times for the summer social work at the Center. As traumatic as it might be for a student and his family, few experiences are more emotionally exhausting than an expulsion for a teacher or headmaster or even a president. Offended parents often fight as if the expulsion were an assault on themselves, on their family honor, and sometimes they remind the world that they are rich, powerful, benefactors: to sever them is to cut off the institution's water supply, to alienate their influential friends as well, to jeopardize the school's very future.

One expelled student was the son of Lieutenant Colonel Walter Bergerie, a prominent army officer, and the boy's mother had pestered John daily to let the boy back. They had had several unpleasant encounters.

So, with Lou Harrington joining us, an evening with the three sisters would both cheer John up and, we hoped, give the sisters one final nudge, if they needed it, to win their brother to our side.

Once again we walked through the beginnings of the little garden within the adobe walls which surround the one-story Albujar house. "We're here to talk about the land. Right?" John asked. But as the three of us were led single-file into the living room, John gasped, "Oh my God!" The sisters already had guests. Seated across from the sisters at table were an army officer and a woman— Colonel and Mrs. Walter Bergerie.

"What the devil!" John gulped. Before we could regroup, the sisters ushered us in and, amidst much hemming and hawing and shuffling and blushing on our parts and attempts to back out the door, the sisters made us sit down.

They explained to the Bergeries, who had been their friends for many years, that we had come to talk about land for the Center.

After an uncomfortable moment, Mrs. Bergerie spoke

up. "Ah, yes, the Center. We know about the Center, don't we?" She gestured to the colonel who nodded but betrayed no emotion. "Our son, Walter, worked at the Center, you know. And I suppose in many ways it's a useful experience for some of those boys. Young Walter, we all know, is not a perfect young man. But what young man today is perfect? At any rate, he has lots of faults, and, as a result of those faults, we know he won't be returning to Cristo Rey next year."

John listened religiously to every word, and replied, in time, that we too—that is, the school—had faults in this matter. But we all knew John wasn't taking that boy back. I figured we were finished.

She went on. And on. John listened all the way. And then she said, "But . . ."

We froze.

She paused, looking at everyone for a second before she continued. "But I believe in this project and I want to help. You know, I'm going to Chile on Saturday with the minister's wife. I'll explain your whole problem. She'll listen to me and he'll listen to her."

Flabbergasted, in the name of the children we thanked them all and clumsily took our leave.

"What in the hell just went on in there?" John asked me. "Was there any reason for all that? What was I doing there?" We stopped at a local restaurant and calmed him down with a drink.

That Saturday, at a luncheon in the minister's honor, the three sisters, armed with plans, documents and maps which Jorge and I had given them, cornered "Kike" (that's what they called their brother) while he was in conversation with the mayor. They rolled out the map, waved their index fingers at the mayor the way a school teacher does in reprimanding a student, and said, "All of it, Mr. Chocano, all of it. Do you understand? All of this land has to be for the children. If it doesn't happen, you will lose our votes next time around. Don't forget that."

Yes, "Kike" and the mayor agreed. All of the land for the Center.

The next day, joined by Jo Marie Burt, a Holy Cross graduate from Meriden who was doing human rights work in Peru and was passing through Tacna on her way to Uruguay, Jorge and I picked out two of the cleanest-cut and brightest boys from the Center, gathered some of the Center's art work as gifts, and set out to intercept the minister's party at a fancy restaurant, Bocchio's, just north of the city.

At the door, security guards searched us and examined the gifts for hidden explosives. A few minutes later, in a flurry of excitement, the minister and his entourage, with bodyguards in tow, appeared in the entranceway. He was not a tall man, about five-foot-nine, rather slender, and balding. And he wore a moustache, which gave him a distinguished look. Then in a second he was gone, swallowed up in a large room filled with dignitaries, officers and their wives, at the end of the hall.

Jorge, Jo Marie, the two boys and I gathered our gifts and our courage and followed him into the room. Suddenly the room fell silent and the guests turned to stare at us and murmur among themselves.

Quickly Chavela stepped forward, broke the silence, and presented us to her brother and his wife.

"What do we have here?" the minister said in the very precise Spanish which resembled that of his sisters.

"I direct the Cristo Rey Center for the Working Child, and the children wish to give you some gifts so you can remember your visit to our city."

"That's very nice. I'm honored," he said kindly and properly as he embraced each boy and asked his name.

The minister's wife said she had heard about our program. Chavela took the gifts—a scarf and a stuffed pink panther made by the mothers, and decorated sea shells made by the boys—and passed them around the room. The officers and their wives applauded.

As we were leaving, the minister of defense told me not to worry about the land.

XV

Family Ties

The Spiritual Exercises of Saint Ignatius Loyola are a series of meditations, contemplations, dramatic images, self-examinations, challenges and formal prayers that Ignatius, the founder of the Society of Jesus, put together in the sixteenth century as part of his own process of conversion, and which he later developed to share with his friends, and eventually with much of the Christian world.

Basically they are a method by which the person who makes the exercises, with the help of a director, by considering the life of Christ and the evidences of God's action in the world, tries to discover God's will in his or her own life. The various prayers and exercises are designed to teach us "indifference"—not in the ordinary sense of that word of "not caring one way or the other," but in the sense of gaining spiritual freedom. This means that if the exercises "work," if we have been really open to what God has been trying to tell us, we have become free to make major decisions without being paralyzed by our attachments, our possessions, our ambitions, or even our loves.

It could mean, to imagine a "worst case scenario" for me, that I could see the whole Center project terminated (perhaps because it was too exhausting a drain on the Colegio's resources and energies), and the Exercises would prepare me to accept this as God's will for me. In that sense, the Exercises are meant to deal with life-or-death issues, the fundamental direction of one's life. They can also simply serve as a quiet time, a chance to calm down, enjoy a week of relative silence, and talk out some problems with a spiritual guide.

Once we had gotten the land, I had to think more deeply about what this meant for all of us. At the same time, the Jesuits had planned a retreat for the Cristo Rey faculty, so I signed up for it.

I returned from a week-long directed retreat in April, during which I made the Exercises, determined to stay in Tacna until I had finished building the new Center. I knew that this contradicted promises I had made to my family and to Jill, but I knew that a lot of people, both in Tacna and those at home from whom I had begged money for these children, were counting on me to finish this job.

I also had a less spiritual motive—my competitive drive. I was in the middle of a cat and mouse game, involving the mayor, the minister of defense, his sisters, city council members and probably some people I didn't even know, over a piece of land, and I wanted to stay around till my side won.

We may never know all the details on who else had their eyes on that barren plot of earth or to what extent various groups planned to use it to make money for themselves. The mayor's maneuvering was clearly tied in with the city council's plans to develop the area with the new transportation terminal and perhaps a number of commercial enterprises. But once it became clear that our committee had the ear of Albujar, the politicians, partly in anger and frustration, changed their patronizing tone to one of outright hostility.

One day the mayor, with a smart, self-satisfied look on his face, insinuated that, according to the Lima rumor mill, Albujar was about to lose his job. Another day Lucho Veliz, the city councilor in charge of the new terminal, snapped, "Look, you guys just can't have all that land. That's just too much. Period. Everybody is complaining about you. We're tired of you. We've had it! Everybody here wants to help you. Nobody's against helping poor children. But these problems take time."

"We don't have a lot of time," I replied. "Everybody tells the poor to wait. I'm sick of being shafted by you guys. Furthermore, we want every foot of it! We're going to set up shops, give people jobs. We're going to make something the whole country will be talking about. Besides, the minister said it was ours!"

But in a sense Veliz was right too. At one stage we would have been delighted with twelve hundred square meters. Now the flush of victory had swollen our ambitions and made us crave the whole pie. We compromised. We accepted the city's requirement that we document exactly how much space we would actually need, negotiated our requirements down to seven thousand square meters, settled, and went back to work.

Meanwhile, news stories about an increase in Shining Path murders and the alleged imminent collapse of Alan Garcia's government increased anxiety and impatience at home. My mother often awoke in the middle of the night fretting about me, and my grandmother imagined that the Jesuits were holding me against my will. In April I let the word slip to my grandfather that, although I had been accepted to several law schools, I would not be back till January 1989.

Jill, who had been out across the country working in the Dukakis 1988 presidential campaign, did not hear of my decision until well into May. She had had it with me. "I cannot figure you out, Jeff. I don't know what you are trying to prove. You don't know how horrible this is for me. Why don't you just join the Jesuits? Then you can stay down there forever."

Just as we were beginning construction on a new outside wall, my mother called. "I'm very upset, Jeffrey," she said. She is the only person who calls me Jeffrey. "You're

Top: Women making clothing for school children. The sewing machines were donated to the Center by the U.S. **AID** program in Lima. **Bottom:** Mothers at the Center's reading and writing class.

just driven to prove something, but I don't know what. But you're missing out on a lot—your sister's graduation, your brother's graduation. Some of your aunts have passed away. You'll never see them again. These people down in Peru, these Jesuits, these people you're trying to help are only passing through your life. They're not your family. You forget that."

Her voice rose as she talked. She grew more and more angry. It did no good to try to explain. Every "but" I tried to interject was swept away and ignored.

"Jeffrey, this is your country. No one works as a volunteer for more than two years. You can't be a volunteer forever. It's time to move on. I think you're under-utilizing your talents and your education by staying there. You're letting us down. To put it simply, I for one feel ripped off. I think you're afraid to return."

When the conversation finally ended I sat quietly, emotionally drained, almost mourning, by my phone. The words that stung were "talents under-utilized." I thought I had discovered talents and resources within myself—to say nothing of what I had learned about the crazy world around me—that I never dreamed were there. But there was no way I could say this and be heard.

The light crept out into the hallway from the office next door where John Foley was working late. He had left home long before I was born and had been toiling down here for over twenty-five years. I stood in his doorway in search of a sympathetic ear. "Well," he said in a rather fatherly way, "no one can figure out what attracts us to stay. No one can understand what it's like here. You just have to accept that and keep going. That's all you can do."

And that's what I did.

But I did return to the United States in June to raise money. Our total contributions for the year had come to $13,000, but the wall we were building around our property would cost over $8,000 and architectural and engi-

94

neering fees would exceed $3,000. Marianne's promotional video had been held up because of her illness. So Bill and Lou agreed that I should fly up to their home territory, California's Silicon Valley, where Bill's pastor at St. Nicholas Parish in Los Altos was ready to sponsor the Center as part of the diocese's Mission Cooperative Program.

I knew I had to come back with $5,000 to make the trip worthwhile, but I prayed we would come back with $25,000. I would stay with Bill's family, and Lou's family would lend me a car. And Jill would fly out and help with the fund-raising. The itinerary called for two weeks in California, a day in New York talking to foundations—and a week with my family. I was both afraid of failure and very anxious to try; somehow I was confident that if I got up in front of a group and told them about the children I would be able to win them over.

It worked. After speaking at the 8 A.M. mass at St. Nicholas' Church, parishioners swarmed around, one woman with tears in her eyes.

One man took me aside, told me he was from New England too, and "confessed" he had gone to B.C.'s arch-rival, Holy Cross. "You've got a good project there. How much are you looking for?"

"Oh," I stuttered. "Whatever you can give is fine."

"No, I mean, how much do you need for the whole project?"

I said we needed about $25,000 to finish the job. He took some literature and left. A few minutes later he reappeared, handed me an envelope, and said, "Give me a call if you need any more help, and keep up the good work."

As I sat in the pew waiting for the next mass to start, I opened the envelope for a look. It was a check for $5,000. I had dinner with him the next day, and over the next year he and his friends helped us with nearly $30,000.

When I returned to Meriden, in spite of our tensions over my decision to stay in Peru, my family and friends welcomed me and gave more financial support. Eighteen months had passed since that Christmas visit home when I was so revolted by the VCRs and jewelry and the general greed of fast-living yuppies. And here I was asking some of them for money.

I was still uncomfortable in a good restaurant when the faces of Agripina, Maria Rivera, or one of the children flashed before me; but the fight to get the land, the realization of how much I depended on people in all classes of society for support, and the warmth and generosity of the wealthy people, who, once they realized how much the poor of the third world suffered, were willing to share their wealth, had softened my righteousness.

As I left I assured my family that this time I really would return by early 1989. But I could hardly blame them if they were slow to believe.

XVI

We Build

"You son of a bitch, what do you mean you aren't going to do any more work today? I just got those two guys to finish the damn hole. I bought the glue. You can't do this. If you don't finish this job I won't pay you for the week!"

"Good, don't pay me," he barked back. "This is no way to treat people. You can't just yell at me and expect me to do what you want."

He ran off swearing. As the workmen stared, I walked over to the thatched shed where we kept our equipment and which doubled as my office, kicking sand in the air and cursing: "These bastards. I'm sick of this shit. Why the hell can't they just work and finish this goddamned thing?"

In the last months of 1988 I was not a nice person.

This latest blow-up had been with Manuel Lazo, our lazy contract plumber who spit as he spoke, often didn't show up for days, and when he did show did sloppy work. I had biked around town to get glue so he could repair the tubing that fed us our water supply. I had just told his workmen, who had wanted to leave an hour early because they had worked an hour longer during the week, that I was sick of their goddamned complaints. It was Saturday, November 12, and we had six weeks to finish this thing.

My days began with 6:30 A.M. phone calls to the engineer and to suppliers I pestered to get us cement, glass, door knobs, tubing, pipe, wire and iron in spite of the country's shortages. I rode my bike to the site and worked there from 8 A.M. till 6 P.M. or later. I was both an amateur, giving myself a crash course in civil construction, and boss—hiring, firing, setting policy—even though I knew little about how to mix adobe or cement and had no more experience in directing men and women than the basic college student government president.

In the evening I stopped in at the old Center until 7 P.M., headed home, worked on the Center's books, fretted over money, called suppliers again at 10:30, wrote thank-you notes until my head slumped and my handwriting grew squiggly, and fell into bed at midnight.

The difference between this construction project and whatever other work might have been available in Tacna was that we wanted this building to be put up by the actual hands of the people who would use it; so, as construction workers, we hired the fathers and mothers (eight men and five women) of the children who regularly came to the Center. In this way our project both had an economic impact on this impoverished urban community and reinforced family stability within the community of people who constituted the Center.

Also, remembering my fight over the farm wages at Ite, we were determined to pay these men and women the full legal wage.

Of course these principles sounded fine, but in many ways they made our task all the more painful. Building the Center took on the atmosphere and problems of a social welfare project rather than a hard-nosed business proposition. There's not much room for sentimentality in the construction business.

Peru's economy was deteriorating daily. And day after day Bertha, who was now deeply involved in every aspect of the Center's operations, would confront me with the tear-streaked faces of mothers of starving children pleading for work for their husbands, even when there was not enough work to go around. The women gossiped and quarreled among themselves and accused us of favoritism if one person, who they thought already had enough food and money to live on, was chosen to work rather than one of them.

When John Foley conducted a para-liturgy for them and tried to tell them that we were all friends, one woman interrupted: "We're not all friends here. Some people get preference. Some get work and others don't."

Bertha replied that she gave work where there was the greatest need. But they kept fighting among themselves.

Sometimes the workers lied, cheated and stole, as Carlo D'Angelo, in that long bourbon-washed night, had warned me.

One payday a father named Jaime, whom I had fired the week before, staggered up to me drunk and shoved his finger into my chest.

"You had no right to fire me, Jeff. There are lots of fathers who work here all the time and make all the money, and I want my chance to make money too. You're a bad person. After all, what's the Center for? To give jobs to poor people, right? And you're not giving everybody a chance for a job."

I tried to explain that the Center did not exist to give jobs; but he got more nasty, and a group of the mothers told him to shut up and go home.

I also had to learn to deal with the national civil construction union, which, to offset price increases of one hundred to four hundred percent in September, had extracted a similar retroactive wage increase from the government, an increase which we, without hesitation, agreed to pay. Still, it was not until I saw Raimundo—a parent who we knew had raised many a welt on his child's back—collecting five hundred intis from every worker as "dues" that I learned that the union had infiltrated our little workforce and organized them.

One morning I arrived at the site to see "NATIONAL STRIKE TOMORROW" scrawled in big capital letters across the blackboard.

"Who wrote that shit?" I shouted. All those in the room dropped their heads trying to act as though I wasn't there. "Get that shit off there. I want to know who did this, and any son of a bitch who strikes tomorrow will never set foot in here again!"

My union-organizing grandfather would have been dismayed. My liberal friends would have denounced me for violating the workers' basic human rights. But I had to build a building and I was treating these men better than they had ever been treated before. And my outbursts seemed to achieve their purpose. Within seconds the board was cleaned. And the next day when the union, mostly unemployed men, marched in the streets, every man on the site showed up for work. No one wanted to fool with the crazy gringo.

At the same time, the other volunteers, teachers who worked part-time at the Center, did not always approve of my methods. As we sat around drinking beer on Friday nights they kept mulling over the whole validity of what we were doing, asking a few days before we were to finish the roof whether we were really helping the poor of Tacna or making them dependent on wealthy Americans.

One reminded me that I had virtually stolen the city's plans for the site. We had lied to the mayor about getting him on American TV. We had tapped into the city's water

Top: Jeff Thielman, Father John Foley, S.J., and friend at an anniversary party for the Cristo Rey Center in September, 1988. Building blocks are in the background. **Bottom:** The new Center building is dedicated on December 23, 1988. From left to right are Father Fred Green, S.J., Jeff Thielman, Father John Foley, S.J.

supply at the construction site even though that was illegal. As civic corruption is measured these days, those were relatively minor offenses. Still we were beginning to resemble the double-dealing politicians we despised.

We told ourselves that when we saw the smiles on the faces of our children at the Center we could swallow our moral qualms. Yet that was basically a sentimental argument—one which wouldn't have gotten us very far in a college ethics class.

When we talked about how I treated the men, they would administer their "boss" a verbal beating: we should monitor what the sub-contractors paid their employees, show more respect for their dignity as individuals, support their right to strike, a symbol of their "empowerment," instead of intimidating them into subservience.

When one dear friend admonished me that we should set an example by paying the highest wages in town, I reminded him that he didn't know what the hell he was talking about because he had never run a major construction project in his life.

Suddenly I caught myself with a weird flashback: I had become the condescending bureaucrat in one of those offices where nobody did any work, glowering across my desk at the naive gringo and telling him to cool down, that these problems were a lot more complex than he realized.

I must also say honestly that on one level, in my third and final year in the third world, I was used to seeing poverty. I had grown hardened to it—at least hardened enough to lay a man off knowing that he would return to his family a broken man.

Each of us—Bill, Lou, Bertha, and the others—acquired our own strategies, our own emotional bullet-proof vests, that allowed us to witness suffering and sometimes death and still do our work. All of us, at one time or another, wept—wept inside and outside—in response to what we saw. I poured out my rage and emotion through work, which was the only way I knew how. But the poverty of the children and their families made it difficult for me to think of anything else. When I danced at a party or went out to dinner, their small huts, their deep brown eyes and their struggles to put a piece of bread in front of each child haunted me.

What was happening to me throughout all this? I was overwhelmed by the privilege of being part of their world. Nothing made me happier than to sit and listen to them talk about their lives and to be convinced that in the long run I was making their lives a little better.

When in August we had come to set the first six of the high columns in place, the workers insisted they could not proceed one more step without their sacred ritual. "We have to baptize them first," they said, "or else we will have bad luck."

So, at their direction, we collected some soda pop, medicinal alcohol, and a kilo of coca leaves. Around each column we stood hatless and prayed "Our Father" and "Hail Mary" while Alejandro, the oldest of our group, genuflected at each column and said, "Sacred land," in both Spanish and the Aymaran language. Then we chewed the coca leaves until they numbed the back of our mouth and buried some leaves wrapped in a newspaper at the base of the column as a gift to the earth.

Later, when the time came to finish pouring the cement roof, we turned that into a festive occasion as well. We rented a cement mixer, called all our families together on a series of Sunday mornings, and passed the buckets of cement hand-to-hand to the roof, the way fire brigades in nineteenth century frontier towns passed buckets of water from the pump to the burning barn. When the work was done we all christened the roof by ceremoniously breaking a bottle on it and eating plates of picante.

In the final weeks, determined to finish by the December 23 deadline, we drove ourselves mercilessly, working each night till the sun disappeared behind the five hundred-foot-high sand dune to the west.

One evening during the week before Christmas, I climbed up on the roof of a nearby building and looked out over what we had accomplished. Beneath me a long, one-story, flat-roofed, gray cinder block 5,630 square-foot structure reached out along the left side of a two-acre dirt lot—including a soccer court—enclosed by a high cement wall. The edges of the roof had been painted a dark red, and little clusters of iron support rods still stuck up where the beams joined—as they do in all the buildings in the pueblos jovenes, symbols that whatever the people have built it is never complete; when the inhabitants have the right combination of money and hope they will add another room or floor. To the south, the spires and dome of the Tacna cathedral stood out against the sunset.

I'm afraid that no one in Meriden would call what lay before me "beautiful." Most likely the neighborhoods not far from my home are zoned to discourage anything so flat, crude, plain. In some eyes it would resemble a garage or a car-wash.

But I thought it was beautiful. I imagined I could see through the walls and into the future: the twelve new sewing machines to be purchased with funds from the Agency for International Development, the six washing tubs for the mothers' commercial laundry, the literacy classes, the art and catechism classes, the fifteen employees, forty mothers, the volunteers from Boston College and Cristo Rey serving a hundred daily hot lunches, teaching, coaching and playing with one hundred and fifty working boys and girls (we were going co-ed) who swarmed in and out of the building, laughing and screaming to one another, who now had a second home, often more stable and nurturing than the first.

At the dedication on December 23, several hundred friends and dignitaries gathered for speeches. John Foley presented me with a plaque which was to be placed on the building:

"The Working Children of the Cristo Rey Center offer their grateful hearts to Jeff Thielman who, following Jesus, came to serve and raised our house upon a rock. Tacna, December 23, 1988."

In the last months I had almost run in fear from the prospect of leaving; I had even asked John Foley to allow me to hang on till March—only to be told decisively that I would have to leave by February at the latest.

I had to force myself to admit that I couldn't be a volunteer forever.

At the farewell party, the kids jumped over me and cried: "Where are you going, Jeff?"

"Home."

"When are you coming back?"

I turned away and bit my lower lip as hard as I could to keep from bawling. I told the parents that the Center was theirs, that they had built it, that they had to set its course. I hugged everyone in the room and thanked them all. I had cried when I left Boston for Peru, and I cried again when I left for home.

Epilogue

As I write this now, a year has passed since I began this story, and I am finishing my first year of law school at Boston College.

As for the friends who graduated with me: Tony is working for his PhD in American studies at the University of Minnesota; Mike finished his MBA at Duke University last May and is now with a financial investment firm in Philadelphia, although he is not altogether enthusiastic about his job; Gonzalo was accepted in medical school but became a lawyer instead and is now with a firm in Chicago; both Jay and Paul went into sales.

Neither of my parents has yet remarried, but each has a serious partner. It means that we spend part of the holiday season visiting my mother, part visiting my father. It was strange at first talking to their new friends, but I guess I have eventually come to accept this. I have accepted their divorce as another factor in the development of my own maturity, my slow realization that the big world is not an easy, apple pie place.

Jill is a political consultant and organizer. She has worked in campaigns for the Democratic Party in Virginia, Indiana, and Michigan, and we still talk and see one another as often as our busy lives permit.

Father Fred is living in a Jesuit community in San Francisco, near his family's home, while he sets a new apostolic course for himself. Meanwhile, they still play the "Marine Hymn" at Cristo Rey.

Sebastian and Herenia have moved to another patron's field where the pay is a little more—but their hut smaller, with wicker walls instead of brick. A new baby, a boy, was born just ten months and seventeen days after the baby I helped bury had died.

In Peru at large, the political and economic situation has deteriorated. Producing coca, the raw material of cocaine, is the country's only real growth industry. The Shining Path has allied itself with the cocaine trade, and the economy as a whole has become so dependent on the dollars generated by the drug trade that it is foolish to imagine that the government would take any strong steps to fight a drug war. One report said that requesting that Peru fight a genuine war on drugs is like "asking a country that's fighting the Civil War and going through the Great Depression at the same time to suddenly take on Prohibition as well." (*The Nation*, April 16, 1990)

The Shining Path are more powerful than ever. Last year political killings jumped by sixty percent, up to 3,198. In the face of this, according to Amnesty International, human rights abuses have multiplied: "torture, mutilation, 'disappearance,' murder and rape have become a hallmark of the armed forces' 'campaign against terrorism.'"

On January 9, 1990, Enrique Lopez Albujar, who had retired the year before as minister of defense, made the mistake of leaving his Lima home without his bullet-proof Mercedes Benz and without his bodyguard. A group of men intercepted the station wagon he was driving himself and machine-gunned him to death.

In a process that has attracted little public discussion, the United States entered the war against the Shining Path by proposing a thirty-five million dollar military aid package to train the Peruvian army to fight the guerrillas. But America has built a base in the Upper Huallaga River Valley, heart of the cocaine trade, where, in a pattern reminiscent of Vietnam and El Salvador, our army advisors help direct the war.

In a letter responding to the *New York Times Magazine* article, "Can a Novelist Save Peru?" (November 5, 1989), Jo Marie Burt wrote: "The article quotes Mario Vargas Llosa as saying, 'People have suffered so long, they are willing to suffer a little longer—if we can show them it is not for nothing.' Easy for someone to say who has lived far away from Peru in the comfort of London for the last two decades; a trip to the southern highlands, where poverty and desperation gave birth to the guerrilla movement, may teach Vargas Llosa that people can wait only so long."

In a presidential election that astonished the world, the Peruvian voters rejected Vargas Llosa's slick ads and free-market formula for economic revival and turned to an unknown Japanese Catholic university president, Alberto Fujimori, who was backed by evangelical Protestants, to lead them. It was also an election where the increasingly conservative Catholic hierarchy backed Vargas Llosa, an agnostic, over the Catholic Japanese—largely because the church fears the growing influence of the Protestants. It seemed, unfortunately, that the hierarchical church was in league with the established Spanish interests, the landowners and the military, with Fujimori, a moderate, as champion of the poor.

There's a standard criticism offered against volunteer projects like ours, and it's a good one. I got it before we started and I still hear it now. It's that personal projects spearheaded by an energetic outsider like me and financed with outside donations usually fall apart in a few years, once the founder packs up and goes home.

That idea haunted me every day for over two years and it continues to haunt me now.

But since I left the Center for the Working Child has flourished. The new director is my old friend and top-notch math teacher, Friday-night drinking companion, and volunteers' best friend, Edgar Durand. On a recent visit to the United States, he commented that if the U.S. has millions of dollars to spend fighting the drug problem, we should spend it in the United States rather than in Peru.

Whereas three years ago the International Volunteers came to work at the Colegio, today they come to work both at the school and at the Center. It provides basic medical and dental care. The volunteers have organized tutorial programs where each volunteer is responsible for one pueblo joven and the Center's families who live there. Some of the kids from the Center have become students at Cristo Rey and are doing well.

The Center now has its own truck—as potent and real a symbol of power in the third world as one can brandish. The new concrete soccer and basketball courts are finished and filled with kids. If plans work, the Center will establish a bakery which, with the laundry and handicrafts, will be a step toward making it financially self-supporting rather than dependent on gifts from the United States.

Finally, the mayor and the Development Corporation of Tacna have given the Jesuits the entire 14,000 square meter triangle. On the new land the Jesuits are establishing a "Fe y Alegria" (Faith and Joy) school, accommodating twenty-five hundred students, as part of a network of grammar and secondary schools in Peru which the Jesuits sponsor but where the government pays the teachers.

Businessman Jorge Llontop is more active in the Center than ever. He shows up for 7 A.M. mass, eats breakfast with the Jesuits, and checks on the progress of the new "Faith and Joy" school which he is helping to build. Father Ricardo, who used to give me a hard time, now occasionally mentions my name in homilies. And the kids ask, "Who's this Jeff?"

As I write this, the March 1990 newsletter from the Center is before me. Bertha Pantigoso has taken two working children from the Center to Lima for a national conference called "The Movement of Adolescents, Working Children and the Sons of Christian Laborers." The two boys, Jose Luis Chino Rivera and David Mamani Cutipa, have organized weekly discussion support groups which meet in the homes of their fellow working children. Jose Luis will attend the second annual Congress of Working Children in Buenos Aires in April.

What was once simply a social problem has become a social movement.

In the newsletter, Teresa Madden, who two years ago gave up graduate school to work at the Center as a registered nurse, has a letter of farewell. She had come to learn Spanish, to experience another culture, to get a handle on the political situation. She was not moved by religious motivation. She was leaving with a deep respect for the Aymara Indians, their love of the earth in which they toil, and an enduring shared agony with the children, many of whom—in spite of the sandwiches—are forty to fifty percent underweight.

She concludes: "I guess I expected to see a lot of this, and hoped to share information I had about health. But I didn't expect that they would in turn be responsible for teaching me, that I would be challenged to develop in ways which I had never known before. These years have been a time of great questioning—of trying to understand the reasons why I do things as such. It was a lesson of what it means to address human need without creating dependency in return. There has been much reflection on all our parts about the simplicity of lifestyles, both here and at home in the United States. How we as a nation waste so much, use so much of the world's resources, value our time more than the welfare of our neighbor. It has been a humbling experience, <u>one where I've been evangelized by these people's faith that somehow God will answer their prayers and make their lives a little easier.</u>"

Since I have returned to the United States, I've seen the film *Field of Dreams*. It's about a young farmer in Iowa who plows under his cornfield and makes a baseball field because he hears a voice that says, "If you build it, he will come." His dream is that someday Shoeless Joe Jackson and the other members of the 1919 Chicago White Sox team will come and play ball there. For months he and his wife stare at the empty field, until they are about to give up and plant corn on the ballfield to save the farm from bankruptcy. Then, finally, Shoeless Joe, and then other long-dead members of the team, begin to appear and play ball.

At the end of the film, the farmer's dead father appears and they play catch. They had fought, and the father had died without the father and son being reconciled. Now the young farmer realizes that the "he" promised by the dream was the father.

The film has helped me understand what I was doing in Peru. I dreamt that if I built the Center the children and their families would come. And they did. But, in a sense, even more than the film, Teresa's letter expresses the fulfillment of my dream.

When I said goodbye to the children and our fellow workers at the Center in February 1989, I told them that I would come back in a few months or within a year or so to see them. But I think deep down I knew this would be hard to do. Right now I can't envision myself going there for a few years at least.

The message I'll carry with me is that a meaningful life means one of helping the poor. And I'll always be searching for an experience that means as much as the one I had in Peru.

Maybe I'll go back after I pass the bar.

Jeff Thielman was born and raised in Meriden, Connecticut. After returning from Peru he entered Boston College Law School, from which he expects to graduate in 1992.

Raymond A. Schroth, S. J. is a professor in the Department of Communications at Loyola University in New Orleans. He holds a Ph.D. in American Thought and Culture from George Washington University and has taught at Fordham, St. Peter's College and Holy Cross College (where he was academic dean). He is the author of two books and over 100 articles.

Questions

1. What assumptions
   did Jeff Corey
   with him to Peru?
2. How did those assumption
   change?